First Footsteps

◆

Maggie Clements

Published by Amethyst Development Books

First Footsteps

© Copyright 2016 Maggie Clements. All rights reserved.

First edition

All rights reserved. No part of this book may be reproduced by any mechanical, photographic or electronic process without prior permission of the publisher.

No comments in this book are meant to refer to, offend or contradict any religious beliefs.

Any exercises in the book are offered as help but are not meant to be taken as professional health advice for any physical, emotional or medical issues. Your decision to use them stems from your personal choice and the author and publisher therefore assume no responsibility for your actions.

The contents of this book are designed to provide an impartial view and the author's opinions on specific topics, allowing the reader to gain an introductory knowledge and understanding of the subjects covered.

ISBN13: 978-0-9954717-0-2

ISBN10: 0995471703

Dedication

This book is dedicated to all those who want to learn more about how they can develop their abilities to live a meaningful and fulfilling life.

Contents

DEDICATION iii
ACKNOWLEDGEMENTS vii
INTRODUCTION ix
CHAPTER 1: Spiritual and Personal Development . . 1
CHAPTER 2: Where and How to Start 5
CHAPTER 3: Our World Full of Energy 9
CHAPTER 4: The Importance of Colour 19
CHAPTER 5: Healing 27
CHAPTER 6: Positive Thoughts and Affirmations . . 43
CHAPTER 7: Crystals 51
CHAPTER 8: Dreams: Does Everyone Dream? . . 67
CHAPTER 9: The Power of Meditation 81
CHAPTER 10: Keeping Joy in Your Life 95
CHAPTER 11: Are Co-incidences Really
    Just That? 103

CHAPTER 12: What Have We Learned
    from Others? 111

CHAPTER 13: Ways of Foretelling the Future . . 115

CHAPTER 14: Astrology 131

CHAPTER 15: Mind, Body, Spirit 139

ABOUT THE AUTHOR 143

Acknowledgements

My heartfelt thanks go to my husband John, who has been a tower of strength, taking the time and having the patience to listen to each chapter of this book as it was written. He has provided helpful suggestions and endless support and encouragement. My sister Ann has also been instrumental in offering guidance, particularly in respect of the exercises.

I also wish to thank Wendy, Cheryl and Anita for their comments on various chapters—they gave me the impetus to continue writing and Sue for proofreading, giving valuable feedback and encouragement. Cath's help was valuable in contributing to the front cover.

My thanks also to Ginger Marks (DocUmeant Publishing & Designs) for her ideas, practical support in terms of book layout and finalisation of the front and back covers.

Pat (a fellow author) generously gave time and guidance in helping me to understand how to get this book published.

Lastly, I want to acknowledge my guides for being with me every step of the way.

Introduction

At some stage in our lives many of us start to wonder about some of the bigger questions about life in general. It is almost as if the day to day lives we lead are not enough and we are searching for some bigger purpose or understanding. Perhaps finding out how we fit in to help us feel more connected and to lead a life full of purpose.

This is the beginning of spiritual and personal development and this book is aimed at such people. I have spent the last 30–40 years exploring some of these bigger questions. Each question answered leads to many more questions and I feel I have just begun to scrape the surface.

People tell me that I am someone who helps people put their feet on the first rung of the ladder of spiritual development—hence the title for this book. It is aimed to be a first guide to those beginning to ask themselves the bigger questions.

Spiritual and personal development is like being a traveller on a long road. Every so often the traveller leaves the highway to explore a side road but later will return to the main path. Following your own spiritual development will be much the same kind of journey. You will wander off to explore topics of particular interest and then return to continue your journey.

The chapters in this book provide some very basic information on some of these side roads. However when you start to explore you may be surprised by the connectedness between some of the supposedly separate strands.

The more I have explored the more I have discovered connecting threads between seemingly separate topics and I am drawing the conclusion that we are living in a totally "connected" world (whether that is physical, mental or spiritual). Each step you take can be filled with excitement and wonder and I wish you well on your journey.

I hope that in some small way this book will help your travels and begin to widen your horizons when you think about and interact with the world around you.

CHAPTER 1

Spiritual and Personal Development

When does the quest for spiritual and personal development begin? I think it is when a person begins to think beyond their own lives and wants and feels the need to explore.

That exploration can take many forms. It may include:

- exploring different religions and other belief systems
- seeking to understand beliefs such as spiritualism or reincarnation
- altered states of consciousness such as meditation or guided visualisation.
- alternative therapies to help physical or mental problems

- wanting to help others by learning some of the healing therapies
- wanting to understand about colour, energy etc.

OR

a thirst for knowledge to answer some of the many questions our world can pose. For example, why do some people have easier lives than others? Why do some people have to endure such suffering? Why do people who hurt others appear to gain?

Whatever the reason or the questions you want answering, I am firmly convinced that when you are ready to begin your journey, something or someone will be there to guide you.

The form this "something or someone" may take may well depend upon the way in which you learn best. We all have different learning styles—some of us like to experiment, some want to watch others and reflect, some want to read, some want to debate or learn from formal workshops etc.

When the time is right either you will feel the desire to go into a particular shop for a book or look round or visit an exhibition such as "Mind, Body, Spirit".

Spiritual and Personal Development

Alternatively someone may just come into your life and you will find yourself drawn into conversations that are important to your learning.

Whatever it is, there is one important point for you to remember—there are no such things as coincidences. If there appears to be something coincidental happening, there is a purpose behind it. Start to be aware and you will be richly rewarded with opportunities to learn.

Your spirituality will grow from within or perhaps it would be better to say, it will reawaken. I believe we are spiritual beings who forget when we come to live a life in our physical world. In my opinion the physical world gives us opportunities to learn both about ourselves and others by playing out different situations. These are situations that could only be debated theoretically (but not experienced) in a totally spiritual, non-physical, world. However this concept links to a much deeper discussion and will not be debated in this book.

CHAPTER 2

Where and How to Start

Start to think about your own learning styles as that will help to shape the kind of activities you plan to undertake and therefore will shape your learning plan.

Get yourself some kind of ring binder so that you can create a "personal development folder". If you get some dividers, each time you begin to explore a new topic you can label the divider accordingly. As you explore different topics you can then put the notes, relevant snippets, information etc. into the particular section and over time you will be able to build a wonderful record of your journey. It also acts as an excellent memory jogger when you want to look back at something you studied some time earlier.

Don't forget to include notes of any conclusions you form, or any experiences you have had—they are an important part of your learning

Begin to see what is available locally. Are there any small local groups or shops that have group meetings? Are there any knowledgeable people who can guide you?

Look out for exhibitions or psychic fairs that might be worth a visit

It is often useful to get recommendations about someone from other people. It may not be a guarantee but it will be helpful. Some people can be very credible and indeed, may be well meaning but they may not be the right kind of person to help others to learn. This may be because their ego or physical needs have got in the way of their ability to move forward. When you are learning you really want people who have a reasonable/good level of experience and knowledge to help you to learn well. This is not the time to learn from other novices.

Be alive to, and aware of, coincidences. There is a message for you in what appears to be a coincidence. It may be that the person or situation is just the next opportunity you are seeking to help you to move on.

Be prepared to spend some time analysing and thinking about what you are learning. How can you relate it to your life and the way you are living it? Are there ways in which

Where and How to Start

you could change your behaviour as a result of what you are learning? Sometimes it is really helpful to use opportunities to practise whenever possible.

Try to keep an open mind about anything you read or hear. It is so easy to let bias or prejudice affect your thinking. Sometimes we "filter" information that doesn't fit easily with our preconceived ideas or makes us feel uncomfortable. Be aware when this is happening and try to move back to an impartial position where you can just judge the information on its own merit. When you then analyse the information a little more carefully it will be easier to judge whether it just feels wrong or right for you.

When you do change your practice and behaviours to other people, be ready to note whether others' attitudes and behaviours change towards you. Quite often as we change our attitudes, so do other people.

Personal note:

At this point it is worth issuing one word of caution. As with anything else in this commercial world, there are people who are only out for their own gain and self-interest. Use your judgement when meeting people and don't be worried about going along with your intuition. Instinctively we often know who we can trust and who we can't.

CHAPTER 3

Our World Full of Energy

Most people don't think about or recognise the role that energy plays in our lives. As you begin to work on your spiritual development, you will become far more aware of the energy flows all around you and the difference they can make to your life.

WHY ENERGY?

We are living in a physical world made up of atoms etc. Put simply, everything that exists, that we see or touch is made from matter and has a vibration rate. Some vibration rates and rate changes we take for granted. For example when we boil a kettle and the water changes to steam or when we look out on a cold day and the rain has turned to snow. The atoms that make up water in these examples have either begun to move faster (because of heat) or slower (because of cold). Scientists have found that it is only when atoms get down to a temperature of minus 273 degrees C that they stop moving completely (this is called "absolute" temperature)

In the same way that everything around us is made up of atoms/molecules, we ourselves are made up of atoms/molecules. Therefore we have a vibration rate as well.

Matter therefore has an "energy field" and as you become more sensitive, you will be able to feel or even see, that field—you can use it to your own advantage. This bio-electromagnetic field is often called "aura". In the past few years, using technology developed from the NASA space programme, Dr Valerie V Hunt has scientifically confirmed that there are two primary electrical systems in the physical body. One is the alternating electrical current of the nervous system and brain which governs muscles, hormones and physical sensations. The other is a continuous electromagnetic radiation coming from our atoms which allows for an energy exchange between people and their environment.

We can use these vibration rates to help us stay healthy (see the next chapter on the importance of colour). However

Our World Full of Energy

we can also learn just to pull in energy from around us. Just by looking around at the wonder of our world—the natural beauty of skies and clouds, trees, flowers, water—we can begin to feel a connectedness. Breathing in energy from the natural world can help you to raise your own vibration rate, helping you to stay energised and fit.

However we can also take energy from other people (sometimes intentionally, sometimes unintentionally) which can be draining to them. In his book "Celestine Prophecy" the author James Redfield describes very clearly the energy battles that can occur when people interact.

He talks about the four strategies (two passive and two aggressive) that people employ to take energy from each other. In a nutshell he describes aggressive people as "intimidators" or "interrogators". In each of these cases people are aggressive towards others and in doing so they can take away the other person's energy, making themselves feel more powerful. He calls the two passive strategies as "poor me" and "aloof" and he believes these are used when the victims attempt to get their energy back by trying to get some sympathy or attention.

It is well worth studying this battle for energy as, when you watch other people, you can see this being played out. It will also make you aware of when you either play these energy games yourself or become dragged into them as a result of another's behaviours or actions. Even when one is aware of what is happening it can be difficult not to get "sucked in" to playing the opposite role.

As you learn more about energy and yourself, you can recognise that if you take an assertive stance in life and your interactions with other people, you can maintain your own self-esteem and confidence level and therefore maintain your energy level without resorting to taking theirs. This is an important aim for all those who want to develop their spirituality.

Another way in which energy can be drained is by negativity. If a person is continually faced with negativity from others, it can drain even the most positive of people. It saps the energy and often people don't understand why they don't have the energy to do what they want to do any more, or find it difficult to maintain the positive attitude they had before.

Healers learn to work with energy and channel it through to other people. The specific types of therapies will be discussed in a later chapter. Each use or channel energy in a different kind of way and at a different frequency.

If you want to become a healer, start to be conscious of energy Try the following:

Exercise to help you build and be aware of energy

Hold your hands with palms facing each other—close fingers. Start with your hands about 6-inches (16 cm) apart and close your eyes.

Now move your palms towards each other and see if you can feel any resistance. Stop the moment you become aware of any resistance (at this point it may feel very faint).

Then start to move your hands apart to about a foot (60 cm) whilst breathing in energy from around you with your eyes closed. Now think about pushing that energy down each arm into each palm as you begin to move your palms back towards each other. See if you can now feel any resistance or perhaps a tingling sensation.

Repeat this movement each time taking your hands further apart. You should find that you can begin to feel the resistance and energy growing and it may be that you will begin to feel this while your hands are much further apart.

When you can successfully do this exercise you will have begun to "channel" energy and be able to intentionally move it around.

As mentioned earlier, as we are made from mass and energy we have our own vibration rate and consequently our own "aura". This is the energy field that extends outside our body. Eastern philosophy talks about this energy field being arranged in a number of layers.

Going back in history, it is believed that people were able to see aura easily but as we have become more educated and scientific in approach it has been trained out of us. You can get it back by starting to focus in a different way.

Exercise to help you become aware of (and see) aura

Look at someone against a contrasting (preferably dark) background. Alternatively look at the outline of a spring or summer tree (in full leaf) against a blue sky. Try to "soften" your focus so you are almost looking past whatever the object is and you will begin to use peripheral vision. You should then be able to begin to see an energy outline—this may look white or silver.

Later on when you become more adept at seeing aura, you may begin to see colour in the aura around people. These colours will change depending upon their moods.

Currently aura energy cameras are available and you can have a photo taken which will show the energy colours in your own aura.

I mentioned that in the past people could see energy auras. This is still reflected in our language and in many older paintings. For instance, if you see pictures of saints in a church or museum, you will see they have been painted with a gold or silver halo. This was easily interpreted by people as showing a particularly "good and spiritual" person.

We have phrases we still use like "this person saw red" (red denotes anger). We talk about people being "yellow" (cowardly) or "green with envy". White is often used to denote purity. These colours are the ones displayed in a person's aura when the particular emotions are present.

I personally think we are much more aware of energy subconsciously than we realise. You hear about people who can project their energy field (some people would describe it as personality) way out into a room. Others quickly become aware of their presence. Sometimes it appears to link with them being used to being on a public stage or in a position of authority—either as an actor, sports person or politician.

Sometimes aura doesn't appear to attract. Have you ever experienced someone walking towards you and you take an almost instant dislike to them? There is nothing rational about that feeling and yet it has happened to most of us. In my opinion this happens when someone has a vibration rate very different to our own and we feel too uncomfortable near this person.

Another way in which we manifest energy is via our brains. Every thought and action is triggered by an electrical impulse—a brain wave. Our nervous system responds to these waves which are sent to the various parts of the body required to take any action. When we have a thought, it

Our World Full of Energy

is also electrically transmitted into the ether. I will talk much more about this in the chapter on positive thoughts.

I have talked a little about energy and the fact that we are "energy" people who have an energy field around us. I think at this point I should mention chakras.

Eastern philosophies believe that within our body we have invisible but very powerful energy centres. These are called chakras and govern the working of various organs or parts of the body. The belief is that they are like "energy wheels"—the main ones are located along the length of the spine and into the head. I will talk much more about these in the next chapter on the importance of colour.

I have tried to give you a flavour of the topic "energy". It is a vast topic and one could spend a lifetime studying it. It permeates our lives and is part of everything we do—it gives us our connectedness to each other, the universe and our power to do whatever we want. Never underestimate the power it exerts in our lives.

At some stage one other thing we will need to consider is protection. If you lay yourself open to energy (particularly at higher levels) you will need to learn how to protect yourself. As with anything else, there is good and evil and you will need to learn about how to protect yourself from the evil spirit levels. Ask the practitioner who is teaching you to show you how best to protect yourself.

CHAPTER 4

The Importance of Colour

In the same way that we take energy for granted and are often unaware of its power, we are often unaware of the importance of colour and the part it plays in our lives.

Each colour is created by a particular energy frequency so is totally linked to the energy we considered in the last chapter.

In effect our eyes do not directly see colour. I don't want to get too technical but it is good to understand a little about the way we perceive colour.

Maggie Clements

In a nutshell—our eyes contain photoreceptor cells in the retina that are responsible for colour vision. Most people have three types of these cells (called cone cells) and each type responds to a different wavelength (short, medium or long). These cells feed information on the wavelengths they are receiving to the brain. They also send information on the intensity of the light. Information is required from at least two of these three cell types for the brain to process and compare wavelength and intensity and determine the colour being seen. Research has shown that people with normal vision need all three sets of cone cells to see the normal range of colours and it has been estimated that a human being can "see" up to 10 million different colours.

These cone cells cannot function in very poor light conditions and at that time receptor rods take over—although generally they only see in shades of grey.

The colours go up in wavelengths and the visible spectrum is red, orange, yellow, green, blue, indigo and violet. At the longer end of the visible spectrum below red you reach the invisible infrared and at the shorter above violet the invisible ultra violet. It is of course no co-incidence that these colours are in the same order as a rainbow as light splits into its various frequencies.

CHART SHOWING THE WAVELENGTHS OF THE VISIBLE LIGHT SPECTRUM

Colour	Wavelength interval
red	700—635 nm
orange	635—590 nm
yellow	590—560 nm
green	560—490 nm
blue	490—464 nm
indigo	464—446 nm
violet	446—400 nm

Coloured objects will absorb some wavelengths and reflect others. White light is therefore reflecting back all the colour frequencies and conversely black is absorbing them all, e.g., if you have a pure white gemstone it will reflect all the light.

In the previous chapter I briefly touched on the energy centres known as chakras. It is believed that the body's energy flows through these centres. Whilst there are energy centres throughout the body, the main centres are considered to be spaced between the base of the spine and the crown of the head.

Once again we are back to the topic of energy and frequencies. The seven main chakras are each considered to spin at a certain frequency and therefore are linked to a specific colour. Again, as they are linked to energy, they represent the same colours in the same order. Below are the chakras, colour and area of the body they govern.

TABLE OF CHAKRAS

Number and location	Colour	Area of body	Sense
7th Crown top of head	Violet	Upper skull, cerebral cortex	Beyond self
6th Third Eye Between eyebrows	Indigo	Eyes base of skull	Intuition/ sixth sense
5th Throat at base of neck	Blue	Mouth, throat and ears	Hearing
4th Heart centre of chest	Green	Heart, chest, lungs, circulation	Touch
3rd Solar Plexus below diaphragm	Yellow	Digestive system, muscles	Sight
2nd Sacral between navel and base of spine	Orange	Sex organs, womb bladder	Taste
1st Root base of spine	Red	Bones, skeletal structure	Smell

Eastern philosophies believe that when all these chakras are open and running evenly in balance (very much like oil lubricating a car engine) the body will be healthy and the immune system will be strong. However if events happen in our lives that cause us unease, depending upon what the upset is, the particular energy centre for that part of the body can begin to run raggedly (either overworking or shutting off). This in turn either means there is an imbalance in the energy flow or that the energy can no longer run freely up the spine. As a result our internal "engine" becomes less effective.

Left unchecked such imbalances lead to physical illness. This is the body's way of notifying us that there is something wrong. Many people try to ignore these signals and carry on. The likelihood is that the body will continue to send signals by making the physical symptoms more severe each time. If people continue to ignore these signals, then severe illness can result. Many physical illnesses are actually the result of some kind of mental unease or issue that the person hasn't dealt with. Sometimes this is because they don't know how to tackle the problem or hope it will go away or in a number of cases, have pushed the problem out of the conscious mind into the subconscious and therefore forgotten it. If problems are "bottled" in this way, the body can become like a pressure cooker. The tension doesn't go away and at some point a physical illness will result.

There are many ways in which to help the situation, the best of course being to recognise there is an issue, find someone you can trust and talk about it so that you can prepare a plan of action.

Our subconscious mind is very good at helping us by drawing us towards the colours we need. This is much easier for women than men. Quite often a woman will plan the night before what she will wear the next day, only to get up the next morning and change her mind. This is because the subconscious mind is aware of the energy centres that need help to realign during the day and choosing a particular colour can help that to happen. It is much more difficult for men who don't have as wide a choice of coloured clothing—only perhaps a shirt unless they are quite extrovert.

Similarly if we need confidence for something we are doing we may well choose black. I have already mentioned that black will absorb all wavelengths and therefore the wearer is able to "pull" energy from other people.

If the problem is of a more difficult nature, it will take time to correct. During that time the body needs some strategies to help it along the way. The following are some short term strategies that will help.

It will help you if you "rebalance" your energy centres so that the energy can flow through your body and help you to self-heal. Rebalancing can be achieved in a number of ways—crystal healing, chakra rebalancing, colour visualisation work etc.

One simple daily exercise to help you stay in balance

Get together a set of small objects that are easy to hold in one hand. Felt squares or small coloured pompoms are absolutely ideal. You will need the following colours:

Bright red, bright orange, sunny yellow, bright green, sky blue, midnight blue (indigo) and violet.

If you are right handed, you should use your left hand for this exercise and vice versa for left handed.

Starting with red, take the object into your hand and looking at the colour, breath in the colour deeply and then out again, visualising the colour going into the relevant area of the body (shown under chakra location in the table)—do this three times—then move on to the next colour and do the same. The action of breathing each colour in order for the same number of times encourages the energy centres to realign. If any are shut it will encourage them to open, if any are over-working it will encourage them to come back into line. Use the colours in the order shown above.

This exercise only takes a few minutes but done each day can help you to rebalance and keep your energy system running freely, which will in turn help your immune system to function effectively.

CHAPTER 5

HANDS-ON, REIKI, TFT (THOUGHT FIELD THERAPY) AND OTHER THERAPIES

"Healing" is an enormous topic. It covers many forms and I know that I can only scrape the surface of a small corner. However hopefully this chapter will give you a basic understanding of what healing is about and, very briefly, some of the forms it can take. It can be as simple as being a friend who provides a listening ear for another person in a time of difficulty or as complex as the most advanced procedures to repair physical or mental conditions.

In this chapter I am not intending to talk about any form of orthodox medicine. I am referring to the many healers using any form of what are sometimes referred to as "alternative or complementary therapies".

Let's break one myth at the start. Almost anyone can heal. Some people may have more natural ability but that doesn't stop other people from becoming qualified and practising healers. There are no requirements for academic qualifications although increasingly practitioners are expected to be occupationally qualified. The key ingredient for a healer is that they have compassion, caring enough about others to want to help them.

One definition of the term "to heal" = "to restore to health or soundness, cure". It is the act of helping another person to feel better, whether that is physically, mentally or spiritually. These three descriptions "physically, mentally, spiritually" give an insight into the breadth and depth of the subject. To explore these in a little more detail:

physically

Helping someone to improve their physical state. This may range from helping someone to improve from their original physical state to helping someone to regain health after some kind of physical setback, accident or illness.

Healing

mentally

Helping someone to improve their mental state. This may range from helping someone to improve an original mental difficulty or problem to helping someone to recover from some mental setback. People are very easily affected mentally by issues that happen in their lives, e.g., bereavement, hurt, trauma, abuse and difficult or unhappy situations. These can result in a multitude of emotions such as anxiety, depression, anger, shame, guilt etc. Some people freely talk about things that are troubling them but many "bottle" their emotions or push them into the subconscious so that they don't have to deal with them. Stress is becoming a major issue for many people (including the young), whether it is triggered by the working or school environment, a pressure to succeed, the pace at which many people now live their lives or a perceived lack of support to tackle a personal issue.

spiritually

Sometimes we carry out acts in our lives that can make us feel uncomfortable with ourselves. Helping someone spiritually is to help them put such acts into a perspective, perhaps considering them from a different viewpoint, helping them to recognise the impact, learn from the experience and move on.

My use of the word "spiritual" should not be confused with the term "spiritualist", which links to a specific belief system and is quite different.

WORKING WITH ORTHODOX MEDICINE

Healers working with any form of complementary therapy have a Code of Conduct that asks them to respect recognised orthodox medicine and where possible work in tandem with doctors and medical consultants. The methods of working with the patient may be different but the confidentiality, patient care and desire to help the person recover, will be exactly the same.

I am not a medical practitioner and therefore will not be discussing strands of orthodox medicine.

My purpose is to offer a brief outline of the practices where I have a working knowledge. I will then move on to provide a brief description of other forms of complementary healing. There are many books, videos and associations available should you want to explore a strand in more detail or indeed explore ways to become a practitioner.

HANDS ON SPIRITUAL HEALING

This form of healing has its roots in the mists of time. Certainly it was described in the bible and is likely to have been used by ancient civilisations.

Healing

It is a form of channelling energy from a higher source. People have different views as to the source of this energy. As a spiritual healer I believe that the energy rate channelled will be at an appropriate level for the recipient. This can be very high level energy (I have been told up to 7,200 cycles per second) sent from very well developed beings (some might call them "guides") existing in a higher dimension.

I have undertaken a qualification and training to help me learn how to receive such energy and channel it through my hands into the individual I wish to help.

This kind of healing is ideal in the following situations:

- When someone is very low on energy, to the point where their body is not in a position to "self-heal" or has used its reserves of energy
- When someone is stressed, very anxious or on the edge of a nervous breakdown
- When someone is suffering from depression

Hands on healing can act like a "battery recharge". Our bodies have an amazing capacity to self-heal. The level of the energy being channelled can provide a swift "top up" so that the body can begin the self-healing process. It helps someone to re-energise and feel able to face situations in a more positive manner. Quite often people who are very stressed will describe a feeling of calm and feel that their anxieties have begun to melt away. This type of healing can be used in conjunction with TFT, particularly in cases of depression, nerve related or emotional problems.

The person being healed will either sit in a straight backed chair with both feet on the ground and hands either in their lap or by their side or lie flat on their backs on a couch. Neither feet nor hands should be crossed or touching. Sitting upright or lying flat allows the channelled energy to flow freely through the energy centres (chakras). If the person is sitting, the healer will stand behind them and lightly place their hands on the person's shoulders. If they are lying on a couch, the healer will position themselves behind their head and again place their hands on the person's shoulders. The healer will ask the person to close their eyes and think of their favourite relaxing location. As the energy is channelled through to the individual they often feel warmth through their shoulders. Sometimes there are other sensations such as a gentle breeze touching their cheek or light pressure on their brow. People may begin to cry as the pressure is released or even go to sleep as they really relax.

During the channelling process, the healer often feels sensations too. In some cases they may actually experience a symptom of the person's problems e.g., physical pain if there is a physical problem or shortness of breath if the person is stressed. The healer may feel the warmth being channelled or see colours in their mind's eye.

Healing

This type of healing does not take long—in fact if the healer channels for too long it can cause the individual to feel very light-headed or dizzy. Although it takes a short time, the effect is amazing and it can be one of the most powerful forms of healing one can receive.

INTRODUCTION TO REIKI

There are varying thoughts about how and when Reiki healing began. Research has shown that it could date back to the time of Buddha and that similar healing practices appear to have been used by Jesus.

From that time until the late 1800s the secrets of Reiki healing appear to have been lost or at best, kept alive by a very few people passing the knowledge from generation to generation. There are question marks as to the date when Reiki was "rediscovered" but no doubt about the person who was instrumental in its capture—namely Dr Mikao Usui.

Over the past 20 years this form of healing has become much more popular in the western world and many people will now have heard of it, although they may not truly understand it.

Reiki is a Japanese word and some Reiki Masters interpret the word as meaning "free passage of Universal Life Force Energy". It is a combination of two words—**Rei**—could be translated as highest spiritual consciousness or spirit and **Ki**—could be translated as Life Force Energy.

Reiki differs from other healing methods in that the practitioner cannot just learn from a book. There are hand positions and certain Reiki symbols to be learned that could be found in a book. However the power of Reiki is passed on from the "attunements" given to the student by a qualified Reiki Master. In a way this is like helping a student to gain a particular healing ability and through the "attunements" the student becomes attuned to universal healing energy. Such energy can then be used in a number of ways—healing (people and animals), distance healing and self-healing.

"Attunements" are used as a way of opening up the chakras so that the energy from Reiki guides can be channelled.

Reiki can treat the whole person creating many beneficial effects that include relaxation, feelings of peace, security and wellbeing. It can be used to remove "energy blocks", be effective in soothing or removing pain, helping a very wide range of illnesses or countering some of the side effects of medication.

If one wants to become a practitioner, there are several steps to the process which are sometimes called Degrees. There are three separate Degrees to become a Reiki Master and a fourth if the Reiki Master wishes to teach others and pass on the "attunements".

Reiki healing can take several forms. It can be:

- a "hands on" healing experience
- the healer can focus on a specific area but not actually touch the patient
- used to scan and heal the layers of "aura" around the patient
- sent as distance healing to an individual or help with an emergency
- used by a practitioner to self-heal so that they are in the best shape to heal others

THOUGHT FIELD THERAPY (TFT)

TFT is a much newer therapy in that it has been developed over the past 30+ years and is continuing to be grown and developed all over the world at the present time. It was created by Dr Roger J. Callahan PhD, who worked for many years as a psychotherapist, but was deeply disappointed by the apparent lack of his chosen profession being able to cure people of their psychological problems.

He had begun to think about new and innovative ways of improving patient experience, including the body's energy system and meridians as used in acupuncture and one day had a major breakthrough with one of his clients. Inadvertently he had made the link between the body's bio-energy system and the fact that thoughts could change that energy system in some way creating negative emotions. At first good results were sporadic but as his level of research and understanding grew, the results improved dramatically and TFT was born.

TFT recognises that when we have a thought it can trigger a negative emotion in us. This might be as a result of a bad situation at some point in our lives or the result of a phobia to something, e.g., fear of spiders, heights or flying. Each time we have the thought, the negative emotion returns and therefore it has been concluded that these two factors are linked in the body's bio-energy system. TFT is a way of breaking that link so that after treatment, one can have the thought and it won't bring back the negative emotion. It is an extremely powerful method of healing, works very quickly and for the vast majority of people.

Research and practical experimentation have shown that a number of the energy meridians linked to the various body organs can act as treatment points and that by tapping on these various points in a specific order whilst holding the thought producing the negative emotion, the link is broken. Once broken it should never return. It cannot make a situation worse, it will either work or it won't.

Healing

Most people find it incredibly difficult to believe that something as simple as TFT can work but I have personally used it with a range of people with differing problems and the results can be amazing. If you have ever seen someone like Paul McKenna asking someone to tap under an eye or on a hand, then you have witnessed TFT because he is a practitioner and uses it alongside other therapies.

TFT does not rely on faith to work. It is immaterial whether you believe it will work or not. It doesn't matter how long you have had the problem. You do not even have to tell the practitioner about the problem you want to tackle, although sometimes that helps because the practitioner can identify the kind of thoughts that need treatment.

You will be asked to explain the type of negative emotion you experience when you have the specific thought as it is the particular emotion that dictates the treatment points to be used. The practitioner will then ask you to hold the thought and say on a scale of 1–10 how strong the emotion is. He or she will then ask you to tap on a number of different points in turn whilst continuing to hold the thought and then ask you if the level of emotion has subsided at all. This is continued until there is no emotion left with that particular thought. There may be many different thoughts linked to one problem and the practitioner will work through them with you until they have all been cleared.

It is staggering how much "emotional baggage" most of us carry around with us and TFT is a quick and non-intrusive way of taking it away. When we are mentally comfortable we are physically healthier so it works on several levels.

It is a fascinating and powerful therapy. If you want to know more you can visit the Thought Field Therapy website or read one of Dr Callahan's books. "Tapping the Healer within" is a useful starting point.

SOME OTHER COMPLEMENTARY THERAPIES (IN ALPHABETICAL ORDER)

Acupuncture

Based on the theory that an energy force "chi" flows through our body along special channels called "meridians". As long as these are kept clear we remain healthy but if they become blocked we become ill. Acupuncture uses fine needles inserted in specific points along the meridians to unblock and restore the flow of chi.

Aromatherapy

This is the practice of using oils extracted from plants to improve and enhance health. It was first practised 3000 years ago in China. The oils (called essential oils) are highly concentrated.

Healing

Aromatherapy can be used in many different ways for a variety of complaints. Its most usual use is in massage. Essential oils should be used by people who understand their properties as misused they could be harmful.

Bach Flower Remedies

Dr Edward Bach (1880–1936) believed that mental and emotional problems were the reason for illness. He identified 38 flowers that appeared to have healing qualities. He made the remedies by cutting off the heads and floating them in a bowl of water in sunlight for a few hours. He divided the 38 plant remedies into seven groups according to the different problems they were being used to treat.

The popular "Rescue Remedy" combines five of the plant remedies and can be used for calming.

Chiropractic

This is a system of spinal manipulation used to relieve low back pain and other disorders associated with the spinal column and nervous system. It involves massage and manipulation of one or two specific vertebrae.

Homeopathy

Homeopathy is a holistic medicine which takes into account the whole person, including their mind, body, emotions, lifestyle, diet, relationships and family history. It is based on the Greek idea that like cures like. If a healthy person takes a homeopathic remedy it will actually produce the symptoms of the illness it is prescribed to cure in a sick person. The aim is to cure ailments by stimulating the body's own healing powers.

Remedies are usually derived from plants although other materials may occasionally be used. The original substance—a natural tincture—is alternately diluted with alcohol and shaken. A drop of the diluted tincture is then diluted and shaken again. This process can take place many times to the point where the liquid is unlikely to contain even a molecule of the original tincture. However it still appears to be able to have a powerful effect.

Hypnosis/Hypnotherapy

This creates an altered state of consciousness which has the qualities of both sleeping and waking. In general people who are hypnotised find that their body is deeply relaxed whilst their subconscious mind becomes very alert. In this state a person is extremely suggestible. It can be used to help to eliminate unwanted habits, fears, phobias and certain illnesses.

Healing

Osteopathy

This form of holistic medicine revolves around a belief that the functioning of the skeletal structure of the body is fundamental to good health. Osteopaths believe that if bones are out of place or joints are inflamed, the rest of the body will be adversely affected. The osteopath will use manipulation to encourage the body to regain its balance.

Reflexology

Another ancient therapy used in China for at least 5000 years. As with acupuncture, the therapy is based on energy flow and breaking down any blockages. There is a corresponding reflex on the foot for every part of the body and the theory is that a practitioner can treat the particular point to break down the blockage.

Shiatsu

This is a Japanese therapy ("finger pressure" in Japanese). It is a manual therapy which involves applying pressure to various points of the body. It is used to prevent disease and restore health and vitality as well as for diagnosing and treating many illnesses.

Yoga

Yoga comes from the ancient Indian language of sanskrit and means "union". It is thought to have been practised in the east for at least 5000 years. It is used as a means of promoting health and spiritual wellbeing by attempting to unite body and mind in perfect harmony. There are a number of different forms of yoga practices including Raja, Mantra and Hatha.

CHAPTER 6

Positive Thoughts and Affirmations

The vast majority of people have no idea how much their own thoughts and comments dictate how their lives progress. As a result they often voice thoughts in a "throw away" manner without realising the consequences. In this chapter we will consider the effects that positive and negative thoughts can create and how these can affect what happens to us.

There is no doubt that negativity is draining and that being faced with negativity on a regular basis can sap our energy, lessening our power to take positive actions. This can easily be proved by a simple test which I have used a number of times in training sessions when dealing with very negative people.

Maggie Clements

Generally we are bombarded with negative comments every day—from TV, press, computer articles, friends etc. Often organisations providing the news seem to prefer the negative story to the positive one, leaving little balance in the diet we are being fed. This imbalance can leave us feeling that the world is a very difficult place in which to live and we can get to the state where we switch off the news or don't read a paper so that we are not depressed by it.

It becomes really interesting when you contrast that situation with the feelings of a good news story. In the UK the Jubilee, Olympics and Paralympics provided many opportunities for celebration. There was much to make people joyful and the response was to make people smile more, be proud of their country and feel better as a result. This is the effect of positive news and thoughts and clearly highlights how this can improve our view of life and our ability to feel good about ourselves and everything round us.

There is no way that one can remove the negativity in our world—but there is a way to keep it in balance with the positive, improving our own perspectives and wellbeing.

Our thoughts can truly have an impact on our lives. During the 2012 Olympics and Paralympics, we marvelled at people's dedication and determination to succeed. When interviewed some voiced an eternal truth by saying "you can do anything in this world if you believe you can and put your mind to it". That sentence sums up the power of positive thought.

Many people have yet to realise the level of power that lies in their own hands. We all have a choice of thinking positively or negatively. Much of the time we don't even realise that we are voicing negative (or at least passive) thoughts. I have worked with a number of people I have challenged for being negative. In each case they have responded angrily saying that they are not. After we have discussed it and I have given examples, they will come back some weeks later saying that I was right but they had not realised what was happening.

WHY DOES IT HAPPEN?

As mentioned before we live in a world of energy. Every time we have a thought, it creates a brain wave releasing energy into the ether. There is a belief that once that thought has been released it will return later as an action. If this is true, then in many cases people will be directly affecting their own lives and could be "ordering" their own future.

This can be practised in small ways to see the results for yourself. For instance, have you ever driven around and around trying to find a parking space? Try saying ahead of time "when I drive in there will be a space for me immediately". It is very likely that the next time you try it someone will pull out of a space just in front of you ready for you to pull in! Alternatively have you ever said to someone "I always get in the queue that takes a long time". If you have, then you have "ordered" the queue that takes a long time! In future, visualise that the queue will move forward quickly and you will be surprised at the difference.

The important point is that you believe it will happen and are not just voicing the words. If you are just saying the words but with no conviction, then nothing will alter whereas if you really mean it and push a positive thought out, then it is very likely that the positive action will follow.

Of course, the same happens in reverse. When people are negative and believe that bad or poor things will happen, that is usually their experience. Have you ever been with someone who says "nothing good ever happens to me". In effect they are "ordering" that experience by the negative vibrations being emitted.

HOW DO YOU BEGIN TO CHANGE TO A MORE POSITIVE FRAME OF MIND LEADING TO A MORE POSITIVE LIFE?

Firstly it is really important to be very aware of the thoughts you have (both the ones you voice to other people and the ones you say in your head). Both will create an energy wave and have the same effect.

Positive Thoughts and Affirmations

Try to keep a note of each time you catch yourself with a negative thought. Immediately you need to replace that thought with a more positive one. It won't be sufficient to think "next time I'll be more positive". You actually need to overlay a negative thought with a much more positive one at that moment in time.

Gauge how many times the negative, or more passive thoughts, creep into your day. Are you more of a positive or negative person? If you see a half full glass of liquid, is the glass half full or half empty. If your description is half empty, you are probably a less positive person. If you are a more negative person, being more aware of your thoughts is the very big first step to changing your life.

You may want to start with small things to test out the theory—and may be amazed at the results. Once you have begun to realise the power of your own thoughts, you can really use them to good advantage.

Some people are reluctant to do the above. People have said me that it feels like they are being selfish or greedy if they "order" things for themselves. There is absolutely nothing wrong with "ordering" something for yourself. If you are a happy and positive person, that will rub off on other people and you will be sharing your increased energy and wellbeing with others around you, in turn improving their lives. You can also share that more positive outlook with others to help them to understand the benefits.

THE EFFECT OF NEGATIVITY ON OTHERS

Earlier in the chapter I touched on the effect of negative thoughts on others. Now that you recognise the power of your thoughts you can take more ownership and begin to be aware of the kind of thoughts you direct towards others (sometimes intentionally, sometimes unintentionally). For example, when you see someone who is dressed in a manner that you find strange or not to your personal liking, might you think "isn't that a dreadful outfit" or if someone is a large person might you think "that person is so fat". Every time we have a negative thought about another individual we sent them a little "secret arrow" of negativity which will drain them a small amount.

When you take responsibility for your thoughts, you will become far less judgmental of others.

If you find yourself being sceptical about this or struggling with the concept, take a short while to reflect on the points made so far in this book. As we have considered the various aspects, there has been a "connectedness" running through the strands and that "connectedness" is "energy". Our thoughts are just another form of "energy".

AFFIRMATIONS

What is an affirmation? The dictionary description reads ". . . a declaration, positive statement or prediction"

Positive Thoughts and Affirmations

Used in the context we are discussing, it is a way of reinforcing the positive action you want to be drawn to you. In other words it is a way of "ordering".

Some people will say an affirmation first thing in the morning so that they are asking for that day or the days ahead. Others will take a longer term view and be submitting their affirmation as a vision of the future. It doesn't matter how or when the thought is voiced. Some people write statements down and put them somewhere prominent so they can read them on a regular basis.

One important point is it must be said or written with sincerity and not just repeated in a parrot fashion each day or as a mantra. Your heart has to be in it.

Think back to those who have achieved, they have achieved because they believed they could and would.

Another important point—do not use an affirmation that will improve you at the expense of others—our lives should enrich not detract.

If you find it difficult to frame a statement or affirmation, another method is to visualise yourself talking to someone after the particular event you want to happen. Visualise the words you will use to describe the success you have had. This is sometimes an easier method for people to use and can be highly successful.

If you are discussing a future event with someone, try to ensure that you use really positive words. If you use a phrase like "that *would* be good" the word *would* implies doubt and that it might not happen—using a phrase like "that is going to be good" is a more positive statement. Including the present tense in the statement is even more powerful, e.g., *I know* that it's going to be great.

CHAPTER 7

Crystals

Crystals have been part of mankind's history for many, many centuries. From the earliest civilisations they appear to have been used to help heal or attain greater self-awareness. In certain periods of history they were put into pieces of jewellery or adornments for clothes or used as talismans and powerful protectors.

Today many people still have, or have recently awakened to, an interest in crystals albeit for a number of different reasons. This chapter will therefore look at the subject from several different standpoints. We will consider crystals as:

- minerals
- support mechanisms and the theory behind why they work

- healing and gem elixirs
- jewellery

CRYSTALS AS MINERALS

Crystals are stunning examples of the natural beauty of nature. Without polishing or cutting many exhibit the most amazing structures and colours. Crystals in their natural state get their form from their chemical makeup. They can be incredibly complex structures and this is not the place to discuss that complexity. Suffice to say that there are so many different forms and the same type of crystal can have more than one form—depending upon the circumstances prevailing when it was created.

Douglas Bullis' book entitled "Crystals—the science, mysteries and lore" sums up the fascination of this subject. He talks about the fact that they are "elaborate arrangements of atoms—some so small that a crystal the size of a pencil eraser might contain 100 billion-billion of them". He continues to point out that "there are 92 naturally occurring elements and that there are more than 2,500 naturally occurring crystals which are made from 25 of the 92 elements".

The forces binding together the various atoms in a mineral are essentially electrical in nature. Known as bonds, they play a large part in determining a mineral's chemical and physical properties.

Crystals

I have no intention of trying to discuss or explain the amazing nature that lies behind their formation, which relates to materials coming from space to help form our planet, how heavy those materials were, heat, pressure, time and space available. There are many sources of information available for those who wish to understand the geology and mineralogy of this topic. Crystals have therefore existed since our planet began to cool and form its current structure.

Crystals can be categorised in a number of ways. For example by:

- their chemical elements and the family they belong to
- internal structure
- form
- habit
- optical properties (colour, transparency, lustre)
- physical properties (specific gravity, hardness, cleavage)

Often crystals are combined. For instance, rutile (titanium oxide) is often combined with quartz to form something called "rutilated quartz". In such a crystal the rutile looks like fine needles running throughout the structure. Rough gemstones such as ruby and emerald are found embedded in other minerals such as zoisite. Small flecks of pyrite in lapis lazuli give the spangled gold effect.

Many people love to collect crystals and minerals in their natural forms i.e. without cutting or polishing. These can be purchased at stalls at mind body spirit fairs, specific shops, markets, internet, specialist retailers, jewellers, antique and collectors' premises and even some garden centres. Their range is vast—from single crystals, to geodes (egg shaped structures with an outer layer of agate and a central cavity lined with a particular crystal such as amethyst, citrine, celestite etc.) to clusters of mineral or combinations of crystals/minerals.

CRYSTALS AS SUPPORT MECHANISMS (FOR SELF-HEALING)

Crystals used for self-healing can be either in their natural form or cut and polished. Cutting or polishing a crystal will not affect its properties in any way that is harmful to its use. If a crystal is heavily chipped (to the extent of changing its natural shape) then it may become less effective.

In any form of crystal healing, crystals are believed to link with one or more of the chakras. Sometimes this link is via the colour of the crystal, other times as a result of its properties.

Crystals

In earlier chapters we considered both energy and colour. When crystals are used for healing these two factors come together. Every crystal has a natural vibration rate and this can be used to help to rebalance a particular area of a person's body if it is out of balance. In other words, it can help to unblock an energy block or increase the efficiency of a particular chakra that has become sluggish.

It is sometimes difficult to visualise an object that appears so solid having a vibration rate and it is important to remember that everything is made from atoms and sub atomic particles and that until they reach "absolute zero" these will be moving around underneath the surface.

Most crystals will reflect light but some crystals have special formations in them known as 'rainbows'. These will include a small area that reflects a coloured pattern resembling a rainbow. Some crystals will have more than one such area. Such crystals are known as "happiness" or "lucky" crystals. When you have them near you or meditate with them, they are thought to bring joy and comfort.

Quartz crystal is a particularly effective crystal to use. The powers of quartz have been recognised for many centuries and certainly appear to have played an integral part in ancient civilisations. They have excellent amplifying qualities and were used in these civilisations as a means of attuning the body/mind with energy and nature in its purest forms. In our more modern world it was used in the first radio sets to help amplify sound. Quartz crystals have also been used for centuries in watches and clocks and are still used for this purpose. They have a number of industrial purposes and now many of the industrial quartz crystals are manufactured in laboratories.

In healing terms, natural quartz has the power to amplify its ability to help the person. It can charge an atmosphere positively and remove negativity. It is viewed as a powerful general healer and can therefore work with any part of the body as well as the aura that surrounds us.

Quartz can be purchased as:

- a single crystal (known as a point)
- double terminated
- shaped like a wand (used for channelling)
- a pendant on a short chain (often used for dowsing)
- a number of crystal points forming a cluster

It is often said that a crystal finds you rather than you finding the crystal. If you are going out to purchase a crystal, you may not be drawn to what may be considered as the prettiest of those available. When looking to purchase, don't be afraid to pick them up. It is important to handle them. Hold a crystal in your hand for a while and see how it makes you feel. If it makes you breathless or feel uncomfortable, then its vibration is not the most appropriate for

Crystals

you. You will find that one crystal usually feels best of all and that is the one you should buy—the vibration rate of that crystal will suit the work you want to do.

Buying a crystal for someone else is always much more difficult as you will not be able to judge the vibration that would suit the other person.

It is important to buy your crystals from a reputable dealer. When you are new to choosing crystals, you will not be as aware of the quality of the item you are purchasing and may pay much more than you should. You may need to ask questions, particularly if you are not sure what kind of crystal you want to meet a specific need. You need to feel you can trust the seller. Many sellers who specialise in healing crystals hold a copy of a book called "Love is in the earth". This is a fantastic encyclopaedia on crystals, covering a huge range, what family they belong to, their properties, how they can be used in healing and the particular astrological signs to which they link. Another excellent reference book is "The Crystal Bible" by Judy Hall.

Once you have purchased your crystal, it should be cleansed. There are different ways in which this can be done:

- Some people advocate burying them in a little sea salt for a day.

- One simple and effective way that you can use for most crystals, as long as they don't contain salt, is to wash the crystal under cold running water. As you do so say the words "I cleanse this crystal of anything that is inappropriate to it and programme it to work with me in love and light". The crystal should then be placed on a natural fabric to dry, preferably on a window sill in the sunlight. If you have purchased a crystal such as halite, which is salt based, ask the seller for their recommendation on cleansing, as such crystals would dissolve in contact with water.

Another alternative is to put one drop of crab apple and hornbeam Bach flower remedies in either still spring, filtered or boiled water and cleanse.

I have encountered crystal sellers in Asia who use sound to cleanse crystals

In addition to the books I have mentioned, there are numerous books and lists of crystals to use for various chakras and ailments. I have provided some examples below for each chakra but they are only designed to give a flavour and if you are beginning to work with crystals it is well worth sourcing one or two comprehensive lists to help you.

Crystals

Chakra Number	Chakra Name	Possible crystals to use
1st	Root	red garnet, black obsidian, smoky quartz, black onyx, bloodstone, pyrite, ruby, rhodochrosite
2nd	Sacral	tiger's eye, carnelian, citrine, smoky quartz
3rd	Solar Plexus	tiger's eye, citrine, smoky quartz, turquoise, pyrite, carnelian, malachite, aquamarine
4th	Heart	green jade, rose quartz, green aventurine, garnet, watermelon tourmaline, malachite, bloodstone, carnelian, emerald, ruby, pyrite, rhodochrosite
5th	Throat	sodalite, azurite, lapis, clear quartz, amazonite, aquamarine, celestite, kyanite, sapphire, turquoise
6th	Third Eye	lapis, sodalite, sugilite, amethyst, clear quartz, azurite, kyanite, sapphire
7th	Crown	lapis, amethyst, citrine, clear quartz, alexandrite, sugilite

The following crystals work with specific chakras depending upon the colour of the stone:

- agate
- calcite
- fluorite
- jade
- jasper
- onyx
- tourmaline

The following crystals are powerful healers and will work with all chakras:

- diamond
- quartz
- rutilated quartz
- zircon
- herkimer diamond (not a diamond, but a particularly clear form of quartz only found in Herkimer County, New York)

As you come to understand crystals more you will learn which ones work best for you. For instance, when I was studying for and taking my business exams I always carried an orange calcite crystal and a quartz crystal. They

Crystals

were near me when I studied and on the desk when I took the exam. I believed they helped me to concentrate clearly. Since that time several others have used the same combination for their learning, revision and exams and all believe that they have aided their mental energy, mental stamina and concentration levels, helping them to achieve their best results.

The following are common beliefs:

- Amethyst is said to be particularly good for those with sleep problems such as insomnia.
- Amethyst, selinite and quartz are very good to hold when meditating
- Fluorite cubes are good "protectors"
- Hematite, sodalite and tiger's eye are good for "grounding"

Earlier on I mentioned cleansing your crystals upon purchase. As they will pick up vibrations when used for healing, they need regular cleansing. If I give my favourite quartz healing point to an individual, it has usually lost its brilliance when it is given back to me. I clean it as soon as it is returned to me and the brilliance returns. Even crystals around the home will need periodic cleaning as they pick up negativity and emotions.

CRYSTAL HEALING AND GEM ELIXIRS

Throughout this chapter I have talked about the ability of crystals to vibrate and amplify. It is no surprise therefore to find that some specialist practitioners have learnt how to use these properties to help people to be healed.

Practitioners will vary in the crystals they use. It may be that one will use quartz crystals working to heal the aura/etheric layers (energy layers surrounding our physical body) and then work to rebalance the chakras. Others may use a variety of small stones, laying them out in a pattern on the patient's body, depending upon the issue to be addressed. In this way the various properties, colours and vibrations of the stones can be used to work together in harmony to meet the patient's needs.

Crystal healing can be incredibly relaxing and therapeutic.

However as with everything else we discuss, it is important that you find a practitioner who is knowledgeable and ethical and one you feel you can trust.

Gem elixirs are believed to be very powerful in their interaction with an individual. They can be created in two different ways (as outlined below) but require the creator to follow extremely precise methods. I must stress therefore that you should not attempt to create your own elixirs by following my simple outline. You would need to read the exact methods, materials and timings to be used before attempting to create such liquids yourself.

Any mineral used for gem elixirs should be pure. The first method is to place the particular mineral/gemstone in distilled water in a stone or glass bowl for a specific length of time. The water is then drained into clean glass bottles which have been sterilised. The second method is to grind the mineral into a powder and mix with distilled water in very specific proportions. The first method will have no direct mineral content. The second method is of a homeopathic nature and will have direct mineral content.

Should you be interested in finding out more, there is a range of books available.

JEWELLERY

As mentioned at the start of this chapter, precious and semi-precious gemstones have been placed into pieces of jewellery for very many centuries. Ancient civilisations such as the Egyptian dynasties show the exquisite use of gold and gemstones—a practice that was followed by many others, e.g., Greek, Roman, Cretan, Anglo Saxon, Aztec

Our modern jewellery uses precious and semi-precious gemstones, some of which are very recent additions, having only been discovered over recent years, e.g., tazanite, zultanite.

Most of us are drawn to certain crystals to wear in pieces of jewellery and it may well be that our higher self is guiding us to a vibration that will help us.

Depending upon whether you have any issues, consciously or subconsciously, that you need to resolve, is whether it is important to wear your chosen gemstone near to a relevant chakra, e.g., as a pendant or earrings. Consider its colour and the properties that it holds. If you are not sure, there are a number of charts available to help you decide. For instance, malachite is often used in beads, which means the nearest chakra is the heart chakra. Green is the heart chakra colour and therefore the vibration is at a relevant level.

One important point to consider if buying either new jewellery which is set or a gemstone in a polished but unset form is "is it a mined gemstone?"

Laboratories now create an amount of gemstones/crystals under laboratory conditions. In this way they put together the constituent parts. It grows quickly and will be perfect in colour and form. The one thing you need to ask yourself is "does it matter that it has been grown quickly under laboratory conditions rather than developed over millions of years in the earth?"

The laboratory version will be perfect in form, unsullied by any impurities or other minerals and will still contain all the properties required of that particular gemstone. The one difference will be that the mined gemstone will have experience of our world over millennia, having absorbed all the various stages. It will have the experience of the planet during its growth. If it is an important gemstone with good clarity and quality (particularly a diamond), seek an authentic and credible certification.

This difference between man-made or natural crystal may not be important if you are just wearing a gemstone because you like it, but may make all the difference if you want it to support you in your life's journey.

Whatever your choice, enjoy your gemstones—they can be an ever present joy.

CHAPTER 8

Dreams: Does Everyone Dream?

According to sleep research that has been undertaken the answer is "yes". However it is certainly clear that people's recall of dreams varies enormously and those with no recall don't believe they dream.

It would also appear from experiments undertaken that sleep is an important part of our lives. Deprived of sleep we become disorientated and unable to function effectively. Yet it has also been shown that when we sleep we are not resting. Physically we move around many times and mentally our minds are incredibly active.

These findings have led many to believe that we need sleep in our lives to allow our brain (and unconscious mind) an opportunity to process all the information it has received during the day and consider the interactions that have taken place.

In much the same way as a computer sorts, at night our brains appear to be sorting, selecting, archiving or discarding pieces of data, deciding whether it is information we need to retain for everyday use, something we might need at some stage in the future, or of no further use to us.

There are different theories about the role dreams have to play in this processing phase and a few of these will be briefly explored later in the chapter.

WHEN DO WE DREAM?

Brain waves change the moment we close our eyes (from beta to alpha). There are two types of sleep—REM (rapid eye movement) and NREM (non REM). There are also various levels in terms of depth of sleep. Scientists have deduced that throughout the night we alternate between the two types of sleep. Initially the NREM phases are longer, getting shorter as the night progresses. The REM phases make up the majority of our sleeping time.

Under research conditions people woken from both types of sleep reported that they had been dreaming. As previously mentioned, if deprived of sleep, and therefore the chance to dream, people become disorientated so it may be that the opportunity to dream is a key reason for sleep.

TYPES OF DREAMS

Whilst dreams are very personal to each of us, there are many common themes in the types of dreams we experience. A few are listed here and the ones marked with * are explored further under the heading "possible purposes behind dreams":

* *Travelling* (by train, car, coach, aircraft, ship or small boat or a more uncommon form of transport such as horse drawn carriage, sledge etc.) This is a very common theme in dreams.

* *Climbing or descending.* (whether by mechanical means such as a lift, or walking)

Flying. Some people dream that they are experiencing flying or soaring over the landscape like a bird

* *Nightmares* (usually reflect intense situations where often the dreamer is considering fight or flight. The dreamer usually wakes before the final situation is revealed).

* *In or near water*

Dreams with family and/or friends (sometimes such dreams involve people we haven't met for many years or who are now living in distant locations)

Recurring dreams where the dreamer is undertaking the same activities each time, faced with the same situation or is visiting the same location

* *Buildings* (the dreamer is looking at or in a building of some kind)

Warning dreams

Being angry and arguing or shouting at people

Being in peaceful or beautiful surroundings

THE PURPOSE OF DREAMS

In ancient times people believed that dreams foretold the future. The earliest record of a dream being interpreted appears to have been Babylonian (mentioned in the Epic of Gilgamesh). The ancient Egyptians believed dreams were supernatural communications and used to seek interpretations. The desire for interpretation has been echoed in many different civilisations throughout the ages and across continents.

Whilst it is not appropriate here to discuss in any detail the more modern exponents of psychology and the interpretation of dreams, it would be remiss not to mention briefly the key contributors as these will have coloured the dream interpretations you may read in books on the subject.

Freud

Sigmund Freud (1856—1939) was an Austrian neurologist who developed theories about the unconscious mind and the mechanism of repression, becoming known as the founding father of psychoanalysis. This is not the place to describe in detail his theories. However it is relevant to state that he believed that the motivation for all dream content was wish fulfilment and that the interpretation of dreams could reveal the unconscious feelings that demonstrated repression and could lead to health problems.

He proposed that there were three closely interrelated aspects of human personality—the id (subconscious mind), ego (conscious part of the personality) and super-ego (high ideals and conscience).

In November 1899 he published a book called "The Interpretation of dreams". Whilst Freud had many followers, he alienated others by his theory that the key drivers were sexual instinct and self-preservation.

Jung

Carl Gustav Jung (1875—1961) was originally a student of Freud but parted company because of disagreements on some of Freud's key beliefs. Jung was a Swiss psychotherapist and psychiatrist who founded analytical psychology. He proposed and developed the concepts of the extraverted and introverted personality archetypes and the collective unconscious.

Jung believed the human psyche was "by nature religious". Instead of the terms used by Freud, Jung talked about consciousness, personal unconscious and the collective unconscious The first and second term may be partially compared to Freud's id and ego but Jung's collective unconscious was a very different concept. He believed it to be the deepest area of the psyche As Nerys Dee describes in her book "Understanding Dreams" *"It contains the roots of the four psychological functions: sensation, intuition, thoughts and feeling. It also contains inherited racial, ancestral and historic memories"*

Jung believed that the archetypes were the part of the psyche that could detach and appear independent to the rest of the personality, playing an important part in dreams

Jung's theories were also used in the development of the Myers Briggs Type Indicator (a well-known psychometric).

Other contributors to dream analysis

In 1953 Calvin S Hall developed a theory that dreaming should be considered as a cognitive process

In 1970s Ann Faraday published books on "do it yourself dream interpretation" and the formation of groups to share and analyse dreams

Dreams: Does Everyone Dream?

In 1980s/1990s Wallace Clift and Jean Dalby Clift identified patterns in dreams and ways of analysing dreams to explore life changes.

There are now a number of websites dealing with dream analysis.

POSSIBLE PURPOSES BEHIND DREAMS

The dreamer may have difficulty in relating the imagery in a dream to their current circumstances in terms of holding a meaningful message. Visual images need careful interpretation as there could be a temptation (as with daily horoscopes) to make the facts fit the dreamer's wishes.

The following highlights some possible purposes behind our dream images but this list represents some thoughts for debate and is not meant to describe definitive research or interpretation.

An opportunity for the brain to sort through the activities of the previous day, analysing the information that has been received from various sources and points that have been learned.

A means of allowing our subconscious "higher self" to pass us messages, either by thought or visual image whilst the conscious mind is inactive.

To help us to solve problems: If we have a problem, especially if it is complex, often people will give us advice to "sleep on it". This may not be such a bad idea as it would appear that whilst we sleep our minds can think through the issue in question without interruption and in the morning often we have found a possible solution.

To forewarn: Sometimes people have warning dreams. If these come true at a later date people will feel they had a premonition but it may be that if they had heeded the warning at the time, no future difficulty would have occurred.

Literal—the dream may appear to be an action replay of a day's events.

To act out another side of our characters: A dream may provide an opportunity to see alternative scenarios in order to shape a future course of action, e.g., scenarios showing results of head v. heart, logic v. emotion.

Creativity: Many inventors, scientists, philosophers etc. have found that when waking from a dream, they have fresh ideas or new ways of thinking about an issue resulting in new inventions and theories.

Sometimes our conscious mind cuts in trying to tell us there is an action we need to take, e.g., one may dream of going to the toilet which can wake one up to the reality of needing to visit the bathroom, or one may feel a pain in a limb and wake up finding one is lying awkwardly.

A visual image of our current stage of life or issues we are facing.

Each of the previous topics marked * are mentioned below:

Travelling

If travel is part of your dream, you may wish to make some notes about the circumstances—sometimes this travel is smooth and uneventful but on other occasions the dreamer is beset with difficulties—missed connections, obstacles, delays or perhaps if you are a passenger others being in control. Dream interpreters believe this is a way of alerting the dreamer to events happening in their lives and the prevailing circumstances, particularly if they are at a period where change is required.

Climbing or descending

Many different scenarios can fit under this heading. Is the dreamer in a vehicle like an aircraft or helicopter, or in a lift? Is the dreamer climbing up or down a ladder? If the dreamer is walking, what is the terrain like? Are there rocks or boulders? Is the dreamer having difficulty trying to walk through heavy sand or is the path straight and easy? Is there any danger on the path? Is it a well-trodden route or is the dreamer walking through unmarked territory?

It is also worth noting at what point in the dream this takes place. My personal experience is that I am always climbing or walking down just as I am about to wake up—never at the start of a dream.

In books dream interpretations on this topic are many and varied but suggest that the dreamer considers what is happening in their life at that moment in time and whether there are any parallels.

Nightmares

It is believed that these can flag up unconscious thoughts, perhaps a childhood memory or trauma or an unacknowledged fear. They can also relate to a traumatic situation that has caused post-traumatic stress. Depending upon the severity and regularity of the nightmare, the dreamer may want to talk to a GP, psychotherapist or other specialist as such issues can affect long term health and wellbeing.

In or near water

This is another very common theme for dreams and takes up many pages in dream interpretation books. If trying to understand a motive for such a dream it is important to make as many notes as possible. What kind of water—ocean, lake, stream, large river etc.? What is the state of the water—is it clear, muddy or dirty in some way? Is it deep or shallow? Is the water still, gently bubbling or a raging torrent? Is the dreamer sitting or standing by it, paddling or swimming? How does the dreamer feel—is it an enjoyable or frightening experience?

Buildings

Another common theme in dreams. Interpreters believe that different buildings can represent traits of our personality or reflect our desires and aspirations. The dreamer will need to consider the type of building, size, rooms visited, state of repair, people we meet there etc.

MORE UNUSUAL BELIEFS

To learn: If during sleep we become part of Jung's "collective unconscious" then there will be opportunities to tap into collective knowledge.

To "travel": Some healers believe that they travel to other parts of the world at night to heal people in need.

To slip into different dimensions: Some believe that we live in a multi-dimensional universe and that sleep frees one to travel through time and space.

My personal thoughts

I do not hold any well thought through beliefs on dream interpretation. However a number of years ago when I made a commitment to work on my spiritual development, I was told that my guides would take me away in sleep to teach me. In a number of my dreams I am aware I am with people, in classes, debating in groups or working one-on-one with someone. Whilst I very rarely remember the conversations when I awake, there have been several times when I have realised that I appear to have gained knowledge I didn't have before.

To illustrate this I will share one small but recent experience. In my dream I had been in a discussion about the connectedness of people with universal energy and I remember asking a question (I think it was to do with telepathy). The person replied with a word I had never heard of but it sounded like "concatanaceous". At that moment I woke up and having repeated the word to myself several times I immediately wrote it down. In the morning I reached for a dictionary to see if the word existed. I found the following entry;

"concatenatus" latin word. "concatenate"—to join or link together, connect in a series.

"concatenation"—a chain like series, as of associated nerve cells or physiological reflexes.

I believe my question had been answered.

Dreams: Does Everyone Dream?

HOW TO MAKE THE MOST OF DREAMS

If you are interested in making the most of your dreams, you may want to take the following actions:

- put a pen and paper by the bed so that you can note images or thoughts the moment you wake up
- keep a dream diary
- log any repeat dreams
- log any patterns or themes e.g., travelling, climbing, same location, same people etc.
- consider if there are any parallels between your dreams and things happening in your life—could there be a message for you?
- There are a number of dream dictionaries on the market if you wish to undertake some self-interpretation.

CHAPTER 9

The Power of Meditation

GENERAL COMMENTS

When one mentions the word "meditation" some people may immediately conjure up the picture of an individual sitting cross legged, eyes closed, chanting "om". Whilst this may be a relevant picture in a few particular cases, meditation can take very many different forms. In this chapter I hope to give the reader an outline of some of the forms meditation can take and the different ways in which it can be used to achieve wellbeing.

Meditation is a practice in which an individual trains the mind to focus inwardly or induce a mode of consciousness either to realise some benefit or as a need in itself. The term "meditation" refers to a broad variety of practices that include techniques designed to promote relaxation, build internal energy (chi, ki, prana etc.) and develop heightened awareness and understanding.

As I have previously mentioned meditation can take many forms. Some people use meditation as a means of answering a particular question. They will ask the question at the start of the session and concentrate totally on that same question throughout. Sharpening the mind to a particular issue can help focus and exclude the many other distracting thoughts that might normally interfere with reaching a judgment.

Meditation has been used since antiquity and plays an important part in many people's lives. Over the past 20 years "mindfulness" has become an increasingly important concept in the west as a means of helping people and is now being introduced into the business environment. "Mindfulness" is about gaining a heightened moment to moment non-judgmental awareness.

BENEFITS

Regular meditation is thought to bring the following benefits:

- can help one to de-stress
- can bring peace

- aids mental discipline
- provides the mind and body with time to be still, helping health
- may help to answer a particular question
- may bring enlightenment if one is seeking answers to a spiritual question

HOW TO START

Meditation comes more easily with practice on a regular basis. When one is preparing to meditate it is important to be comfortable—wear comfortable clothing and sit in a way that feels right for you. Whatever position you choose—on the floor on cushions, propped against the wall or in a chair—you will need to be able to maintain that position without pain for a length of time. It therefore needs to be comfortable without effort and ideally your back should be straight so that the energy can run up and down your spine freely.

The location you choose is also important. Meditation is about "shutting off" from the everyday world, so you will need to ensure that you cannot be disturbed by sounds, particularly a sudden sound such as a telephone/mobile or door bell ringing. It can be very a difficult experience if a meditation is suddenly broken and one is returned to reality with a jolt.

When people first try to meditate, many find it extremely difficult to "still" their minds. We are used to having huge numbers of little thoughts flitting into our brains and to suddenly expect to be able to keep these thoughts away is not realistic. Emptying and disciplining one's mind to be peaceful takes much work and practice. Some beginners like to concentrate on a particular object, phrase, word or sound in order to help them.

Others prefer to use some form of visualisation. This can be undertaken one-on-one or in a group with a person guiding one through the visualisation or alternatively via an audio or DVD. Often this visualisation will take the form of walking one through an area and then leaving one for an appropriate time to meditate before bringing one back to the present. This can be a very powerful and effective form of meditation as the mind has something to focus upon at the start and it gently moves one into a more peaceful frame of mind before the period of quiet reflection.

If you are buying audio tapes or DVDs, look to see if they contain something called "subliminals". Subliminals are embedded messages that will be picked up by your brain and will contain suggestions during your meditation. At a conscious level you will not be aware of these messages in any way but your brain will respond to them so you need to understand what they are and how they will be used. For some people they can enhance the meditation experience.

The Power of Meditation

A number of people find that holding a crystal whilst they meditate helps them to improve the experience by raising vibration for greater concentration. Selenite can be a particularly powerful crystal to use in this way. Others may include blue lace agate, fluorite, quartz, amethyst, azurite, smoky quartz, rhodochrosite and celestite.

If you have an active mind, it may not be easy to "switch off" when you first begin to meditate. If this happens and thoughts pop into your head, just acknowledge them and let them go—don't dwell on them. I have a very active mind and often I will get my mind still for a few seconds only to have the thought come in "I have managed not to have a thought for . . . seconds". I have now learnt to just let it happen and move on rather than worrying that I cannot maintain a still mind.

Unless you are good at emptying your mind and being totally still, it is often better to start with some kind of visualisation as it provides the opportunity to concentrate all your thoughts on what is being said and what you are being asked to do. Using a colour visualisation or some form of relaxation exercise can help to set the tone for the meditation session.

A FEW DIFFERENT MEDITATION TECHNIQUES

Simple meditation

Choose a quiet spot where you won't be disturbed.

Sit quietly in a comfortable position (either in a chair or with your back to a wall) with your back straight between base of spine and head

Pick a focus word or short phrase to use that is part of your belief system.

Close your eyes.

Begin by relaxing all muscles in turn from head to feet (one good way is to tense the particular muscle, hold for a few seconds and then release). Do this for all main muscles, remembering to include arms and hands.

Then breathing slowly and gently repeat your focus word or phrase as you exhale.

Don't worry about thoughts that intrude, acknowledge and let them go

Continue for 10–20 minutes

Then sit quietly for a minute, open your eyes and adjust. Do not try to stand immediately.

Mindfulness (insight meditation)

This is the art of becoming deeply aware of the present moment and leads to fully experiencing what is happening in the here and now. It is a technique that tunes out all the normal noise in one's head and allows one to really "see" or "sense"

In becoming fully aware of each moment, you become the impartial witness. You are just observing—accepting and non-judgmental . It allows those who use the technique to respond to any issue in a less impulsive and more measured way.

Begin with a simple action, perhaps drinking or eating something or stroking a pet. Fully concentrate on your actions, observing and feeling what you are doing to the exclusion of everything else. You will begin to be aware of sensations that are normally ignored in our rushed and often superficial attention.

In this activity if a thought comes into mind, dismiss it and return to the total concentration of your actions. This can promote a very real feeling of calm and serenity and help one to appreciate the beauty or intricacy of actions so normally taken for granted.

Transcendental meditation (TM)

This kind of meditation has become increasingly popular since the late 1950s. Each person is given a word or phrase by their instructor which is personal to them and they promise never to divulge. They are then asked to sit with eyes closed and repeat the mantra continually for 20 minutes daily.

This mantra focuses the mind on a single idea representing the "oneness" of the universe.

Research has shown that during TM the body gains a deeper state of relaxation than during normal rest and that there are many long term benefits in terms of mental and physical health.

Journey meditation

Choose a quiet spot where you won't be disturbed.

Sit quietly in a comfortable position (either in a chair or with your back to a wall) with your back straight between base of spine and head

Take a few slow breaths to begin the relaxation process.

Find some place where you feel totally safe, happy and calm. This might be a favourite place to visit or just a mental picture of the type of environment you enjoy. Some people will use a quiet beach, peaceful woodland scene or being near water of some kind (a tinkling stream or lake).

In this place you can just observe or walk—whatever is right for you. Just enjoy being part of the scene and become totally absorbed into it.

Try to allow yourself at least 10 minutes once a day for this activity and it will help you to feel totally peaceful and energised.

A BRIEF LOOK AT LINKS BETWEEN MEDITATION AND VARIOUS RELIGIONS/ BELIEF SYSTEMS

Buddhism

Meditation is pursued as part of the path towards enlightenment and Nirvana. There are two paramount mental qualities that come from meditation, namely serenity or tranquillity and insight. Through serenity one can release hindrances and insight is developed in order to gain wisdom.

Christianity

Meditation is a form of prayer in which a structured attempt is made to get in touch and deliberately reflect upon, the revelations of God. Focus on specific thoughts. It aims to higher the personal relationship based on the love of God that marks Christian communion.

*Hinduism**

Meditation is known as dhyana (a Sanskrit word meaning journey or movement of the mind). One withdraws one's mind and senses from the distractions of the world to contemplate upon a chosen object or idea with concentration.

The mind and body has to be brought together to function as one harmonious whole.

In dhyana people gain insightful awareness, understanding the nature of things. In Hindu philosophy the mind (manas) is viewed as a receptacle (dhi) into which thoughts pour back and forth from the universal pool of thought forms. In Hindu tradition the human mind has the creative potency of God. You become what you think. You are the sum total of your thoughts and desires and these influence the course of your life here and hereafter. All your mental actions are part of your karma as much as any physical action.

taken from the hinduwebsite.

Islam

Both Sunni and Shia Muslims adhere to the practice of "salat" which is the act of reciting devotional prayers five times daily. They believe this is a central tenet of Islamic faith. There are question marks about the acceptability of any form of meditation and whether it is considered to be acceptable appears to depend upon the person themselves, their reason for undertaking it and their interpretation of its acceptance in the Koran.

Sufism—Sufi Islam is a wide definition referring to Islamic groups who do not adhere in their entirety to either Sunni or Shia practices. For such people meditation other than "salat" is often a central practice. By meditating Sufis aim to reach awareness of the oneness with the universe, believing that in doing so they can attain fundamental truths that are within them but often remain hidden. Meditation directs all breathing controls and the repetition of holy words.

Jainism

Meditation aims to take the soul to complete freedom. It aims to reach and to remain in the pure state of the soul which is able to be pure consciousness beyond any attachment or aversion. Mantra chanting is an important part of Jainism—can be out loud or silently in the mind. Breathing exercises are undertaken to strengthen vital energy.

New Age

Often influenced by eastern philosophy, mysticism, yoga, Hinduism and Buddhism. In the west meditation found its mainstream roots from the social revolution of 1960s and 1970s when some young people rebelled against traditional belief systems. Followers tried to blank out the mind and release conscious thinking. They often used repetitive chanting of a mantra or focused on an object such as a candle flame to aid meditation.

The Power of Meditation

Sikhism

Encourages quiet meditation focusing one's attention of the attributes of God. Sikhs believe there are 10 energy chakras—the top one is called Dasam Duaar. When one reaches this stage through continuous practice, meditation becomes a habit that continues whilst walking, talking etc. At this level one experiences absolute peace and tranquillity inside and outside the body. Singing hymns can be seen as one of the most beneficial ways of aiding meditation.

Taoism

Seeks the generation, transformation and circulation of internal energy, which can then be applied to other activities. Taoist meditation seeks jing (quiet, stillness, calm) and ding (concentration, focus). The purpose of stillness, both mental and physical, is to turn attention inwards and cut off external sensory input. Within that stillness, the meditator concentrates the mind and attention on the breath, in order to develop what is called "one pointed awareness" which is a totally undistracted and undisturbed state of mind permitting intuitive insights to arise.

CHAPTER 10

Keeping Joy in Your Life

This is a really simple statement. In reality it represents something that, for the vast majority of people, can be extremely difficult to maintain. *Joy* is a lovely word—sadly not used very often in our daily lives.

One definition of joy is "A lively emotion of happiness. Anything which causes delight."

Sometimes when I begin to work with people who are struggling or have health problems of some kind I will ask "what gives you joy in your life?" Often they will just stare at me with a surprised look on their face, and then think for a while and sadly sometimes the answer is "nothing".

For these people life appears to have become one long chore with no rest or let up from the daily grind or pressure—nothing to relieve the stress.

Joy can be experienced in so many different ways. Sometimes very small things can bring infinite pleasure. One thing is certain—joy is an intensely personal sensation and will result from your view on life and what is important to you as an individual. It may link to your values, pleasures, beliefs, family or activities. A little later in the chapter we will explore some of these in more detail.

So, why is it important to ensure that there is a measure of joy in your life?

As we have already learnt in the preceding chapters, a measure of positive energy is vital to health, balance and wellbeing. It would appear at the present time that for many people there is more negative energy being directed to them. Joy will relieve stress and negativity.

As mentioned before, the media in all its forms seems to have moved away from any kind of balance in their reporting of world stories. As a result we are continually bombarded by negativity. Earlier in this book we discussed the way in which negativity is draining and this continual imbalance in the information being presented to us can have the effect of draining our energy. It must have the same effect on the news readers so no wonder they smile and comment when finally there is a good news story or something that offers light relief. I now come across many people who no longer watch the news on television because they say they don't want to be depressed.

We can almost be forgiven for thinking that the world is a dreadful place in which to live—and indeed for people, particularly in countries facing war, persecution, misused power, poor administration and management and greed it must feel that way.

However in many countries, there are many, many good things happening. There are people achieving amazing things, others being beacons by the way in which they react to difficulties or help other people. It is immaterial whether this is on a one-on-one home care basis, a battle with a personal illness, being an example to others or a wider offering supporting complete communities. In reality in such areas negative and positive experiences are probably in a balance but just not reported in that proportion.

Keeping a measure of joy in your personal life is a way of counteracting this negativity and providing you with the necessary energy and drive to lead a full and happy life. Sometimes we can become so caught up in all the routine of trying to live from day to day, work, eat, sleep and work again that there seems little time for anything else. Routine in itself is passive and can become exceedingly boring and de-energising. Certain people may find routine gives them a measure of security and acts as a comfort blanket but for many it provides the kind of desensitisation where life becomes more of an existence. Tasks that we do often can easily become a chore. If this happens, look at how you can make it feel a bit more positive or alternatively do you really have to continue to do this task? I've put a little message on my computer as a screensaver and it reads *"keep joy in your heart in everything you do"*.

So, how to break negativity? Even if it is only for one minute of a day, begin to focus on one thing that brings you pleasure. Concentrate totally on that particular thing, mentally *noting* and really *feeling* what makes it so good. If possible then, after the first week, try to spend twice a day focusing on things etc. Soon it will become a habit and a great antidote for negativity.

What kind of things bring people pleasure? Well it can be just about anything. The following are just some examples under topic headings.

Weather

A beautiful morning—a sunny day—blue sky and fluffy white clouds—sunrise—sunset—warmth—a crisp snowy day—seeing the start of a season (spring flowers or autumn colours)

Pets

Walking them—stroking them—playing with them—having them come to greet you when you first get home—receiving affection from them—interacting with them (e.g., riding or grooming horses)—breeding them

Touch

Feeling pleasure at a particular texture like fur or velvet, touch as a means of communication (particularly if poorly sighted)—holding hands or linking arms to show affection

Sound

Music—bird song—water of some kind (e.g., waterfall, river, waves crashing on a beach)

Smells

Food (fresh baking or cookery)—freshly ground coffee—flowers—newly mown grass if you like the countryside—particular perfumes or oils that awaken the senses

Food

The pleasure of looking at well-presented food—trying different food sensations from different cultures—savouring a favourite food or a special treat—preparing it for people—experimenting with flavours

Family and friends

Spending time with people whose company you enjoy—being reunited with people you haven't seen for a while—sharing good company, conversation and similar interests—a new addition to the family—preparing for an event such as birthday, Christmas etc.

Peace and tranquillity

Silence—the peace of a quiet place—chance to have some time on one's own

Creativity

Being able to create something—perhaps an art form (painting, drawing, photography, sculpting, writing)—making clothes or gifts for people—inventing things

Gardens and ponds

Creating a haven—choosing beautiful plants—appreciating shape, texture and colour—producing vegetables and fruit for the table—encouraging butterflies, bees and other forms of nature into the garden to help the environment—feeding and caring for fish

Country or wild animals

Watching in a zoo or park—watching wild animals that come into your garden or you see in the surrounding countryside (especially if they are more unusual). Creating the kind of environment where animals feel safe and welcome

Birds

Attracting birds to watch them feed—looking out for different species—interacting with them as they become more tame (e.g. robin coming to feed when you garden, birds coming to seek food)—having a pet bird or birds

Sport and exercise

For many people playing a sport or doing some form of exercise/gym work can become all-consuming in terms of requiring complete concentration. This in its own way can be a great relief from stress. For others following a sport can be just as absorbing and satisfying.

Travel and holidays

Opportunities to visit exciting new places—visit sun-drenched beaches with clear turquoise water—see incredible buildings—learn about history—learn about totally different cultures—see new cities and new countries—try out aircraft, ships, trains

Shopping

For some people retail therapy is an absolute must—whether it is a particular type of purchase (shoes or handbags appear to be a "must" for some women), browsing on the internet or wandering around shopping centres and charity shops.

FINAL THOUGHTS

I've tried to outline some things that give people pleasure but as mentioned earlier, these really are endless. The important thing is to create sufficient regular opportunities to allow yourself some "me" time. This will help you to become more aware of the pleasurable things in life that help to balance and provide more energy and wellbeing.

CHAPTER 11

Are Co-incidences Really Just That?

There are many, many times in our lives when things happen and we say "wasn't that a co-incidence"—for example people we are thinking about whom then get in touch with us by telephone or email or we bump into them in the street. We tend to think of these events as totally random and just something that has happened. However it may be helpful to adjust that thinking and view such happenings from a different perspective.

What if these events are not co-incidental but are intentional? Sometimes when we are trying to learn a particular point, someone comes into our life at just the right time to provide the answer. Think back—are there any events you previously thought were co-incidental that were actually designed to give you a message that was important to you at that moment in time? Think about what you were seeking when the co-incidence happened—did it actually answer a question in your mind, give you certain knowledge when you needed it or even help you to make a decision?

There is a school of thought that says what appear to be co-incidences are in fact opportunities. They are opportunities for us to learn something that will help us move forward at a time when we need it. Most of the time we do not recognise the significance of the co-incidence so the opportunity to learn can be lost. However it is possible to become much more open and aware of these and as a result, take advantage of these chances.

I believe that there are different types of co-incidences. The kind where you are thinking about someone and then they pop up or get in touch may be explained by the fact that you have a mental link to that individual and your brainwave triggers an electrical response in their brain. Thus the closeness of the thought patterns has provided the so-called co-incidence. This is usually a pleasurable experience in that it gives an opportunity for communication that has sub-consciously been sought. This is perhaps less of a co-incidence than a "cause and effect".

However there appears to be another kind of co-incidence that can happen to people and often such events can have a profound influence on the person's life. These are often

Are Co-incidences Really Just That?

much more subtle and we can be totally unaware that we are being "guided" in any way. Such events can be many and varied but it would probably be helpful to the reader if I provide one or two examples of the kind of events I have in mind.

It may be that someone is asking themselves a particular question and is having difficulty in arriving at a conclusion. They may have puzzled for some time or feel that are in a "grey" state about the action to take. At that point a person, book, example or event may just come along that gives them an idea of a way forward. There is no apparent link between the two things and yet one has helped the other.

I heard of a really interesting example just the other day on a local TV programme where they were interviewing someone who does the most beautiful sign-writing, runs his own business and is now more in demand than ever. He was explaining to the interviewer that he had left school at 15 with no idea of what he wanted to do. He walked out of the school building and started to walk home. A van stopped and the driver offered him a lift. The van driver was a sign-writer who was looking for a new person to work with him. He offered the 15 year old the chance of working with him and beginning a career. The young boy accepted and his sign-writing career began. One could just say that was a co-incidence or alternatively that the right person came along at just the right moment to provide a direction and future for someone who had been aimless and couldn't wait to leave school with no idea of what he wanted to do.

One day I went off to a business breakfast. I was talking to two other professional ladies and we were so engrossed in our business conversation that we were the last to move through to the breakfast area. There were only three places left—one on a large table and two on a small table in the middle. One lady and I took the small table and within a very short time she mentioned the ring I was wearing. We began to talk about crystals and discovered that we both had a love of crystals, healing and a number of other topics. We spent the whole breakfast sharing ideas and at the end she said how helpful our conversation had been. Within one week that meeting lead to an opportunity to go along to a new open circle that was setting up in Royston where I met a masseuse who is also an alternative healing practitioner.

Within a very few weeks of that business breakfast one of the ladies I had met asked me whether I would like to join her in a visit to Royston Cave. I had previously wanted to visit but never found the time. We went together to the last opening of the year (it shuts end September—April) I was captivated and immediately vowed to learn to become a cave guide. This ambition was realised within one year and I now guide on a regular basis. As a result I now get a chance to talk to a wide range of people with

Are Co-incidences Really Just That?

different ideas including people who are interested in the Knights Templar (one of my reading hobbies), spiritual people who come because they believe the cave has special healing powers due to its location on the crossing of two important ley lines and those who understand Masonic practices. Conversations are fascinating and help me learn so many different views which give me a chance to develop my own thinking.

The above examples of meetings and conversations could be classed as co-incidences or could be classed as an opportunity to meet like-minded people, open up new development opportunities and allow one to move forward. I would choose to think it is the latter.

The best way to make the most of these opportunities is to be mindful. Look out for small signs or even people or things that attract you. It might mean you walk into a shop you weren't intending to visit or smile at a stranger you feel drawn to. It might be something as simple as missing a bus or other form of transport and catching a later one where you meet an individual who is important to you or reading a chance poster.

You may ask, if these are not coincidences then how do they happen—who helps them to happen? Some people believe that we have spirit beings (we may call them guides, gatekeepers, angels etc.) who are watching over us all the while. They will not interfere unless asked but they can watch our development and help when we are seeking guidance by arranging some kind of support. Other people believe that our lives are mapped out before we live them and that we have "contracted" with certain people to provide us with certain experiences, knowledge, support etc. If this is the case then it is believed that when we reach a certain stage where we need a particular type of support, the person who contracted to provide that will arrive on the scene.

The co-incidence can revolve around an object. There are a number of instances of people having white feathers fall near them and a number believe that these are a symbol of angels, a guardian angel or the spirit of someone who has recently died and is trying to provide comfort. If you look on the internet you can read about a range of examples from individuals and certainly Gloria Hunniford has written some books on the subject of her personal experiences.

In a wider context, there are times in history when it seems like the person with the right energy, knowledge and drive has arrived on the scene at just the right time to intervene in a positive manner. Hence the phrase, "Cometh the moment, cometh the man."

A more controversial question is the belief that animals, birds and insects can also be bringers of messages. Some people believe that if such a creature comes into our lives,

Are Co-incidences Really Just That?

it has a message for us which is pertinent to the current situation. I have a number of books giving interpretations of the kind of messages these creatures can bring. Personally at this moment in time I am still debating whether I believe they are intended messengers. My reasoning says as all such creatures are made up of the same atoms and energy as ourselves they are connected to the universe in just the same way. It is possible they may have the same links and I would be wrong to dismiss the idea as an impossibility.

Certainly the ancient civilisations believed in such totems and in his book "Celestine Prophesy" James Redfield talks about the need to be aware when nature in any form is providing guidance.

It is a fascinating topic and one that will clearly have people divided in their thinking.

CHAPTER 12

◆

What Have We Learned from Others?

I firmly believe that in this life we meet people or cross paths with people at a time that is appropriate for us to learn something. If we are not in a state of awareness, sometimes these opportunities pass us by and we don't recognise the significance.

As we learned in the preceding chapter on co-incidences, the timing of such meetings can be very valuable and give us an opportunity to move forward in some direction or increase our knowledge on a particular topic.

Sometimes what appear to be chance meetings give someone an opportunity to totally change their life's direction or career—they might think of it as just being 'in the right place at the right time'. I would argue there should be a synchronicity to everything we do and it is in recognising the message, or having the courage to grasp the opportunity, that gives us the chance to move forward in some way. Too often we give it half a passing thought and then shrug and the moment is lost. It may be some time before it returns and that lost opportunity could set us back some months or even years.

The kind of messages we receive may not always be verbal or even appear to be directly aimed at us at all. Sometimes by just being near someone else and observing their behaviour there is a learning opportunity that we can benefit from and adapt to suit ourselves. I had the perfect example of such a situation on a past holiday cruise.

I try to actively listen to people but I sometimes have a problem in that in my desire to be part of a conversation I jump in to say something before another person has finished speaking. I know it is a very impolite thing to do and have been working to try to stop myself doing it. I met, and had the opportunity to observe, a person whose active listening skills were stunning. This person is able to devote all their attention to looking at and listening to, the person who is speaking. They will nod or smile as a means of acknowledging but do not interrupt in any way. Once the person has finished speaking they will quietly reply. It looks effortless and makes the person they are listening to

What Have We Learned from Others?

feel valued and respected for their words. It is an object lesson for me and a great learning opportunity to adopt a similar behaviour and techniques. The person in question was not aware that I was learning from them but I knew that this was an opportunity for me and one that I could model and improve.

Sometimes we can see other behaviours that give us chances to learn. You see it in interactions that happen around you. People can enter a room or area and bring an atmosphere with them. This can be positive or negative. Someone comes in and smiles—immediately people respond by smiling back and the whole atmosphere can lighten. Conversely if someone comes in with a frown on their face and grumbles, the atmosphere becomes heavier and more negative. One person's mood and behaviour can be infectious. We are quite easily affected by the people around us. I wonder if we ever stop to think of the responsibility each of us has not to "mess up" someone else's atmosphere and environment.

There are times when the messages are much more direct, verbal and aimed specifically at us an individual. We are introduced to someone or appear to have a chance meeting with someone and there is a direct opportunity to move forward. The role of teacher may be recognised in which case there are many chances to ask questions, hold some quality conversations, and make the most of the opportunity to learn. Sometimes the balance is more equal and each is able to help the other move forward in a reciprocal manner.

I'm sure you have noted that throughout this short chapter I have emphasised the chance to learn. I am sure that many of our interactions with others are about learning—we just need to notice and remember to give ourselves a chance to allow time to make the best of them.

CHAPTER 13

Ways of Foretelling the Future

Trying to foretell the future has been important to people throughout different civilisations. In ancient times leaders would consult oracles before going to war in the hope that they would receive a positive message about the outcome of the forthcoming battle. Ancient people have read signs in nature and the skies as portents of good or disasters and in the New Testament of the bible, a star is seen as heralding a momentous event and the story says people followed it to find the baby Jesus

For many of these races in the past, the wish to know the future linked to the country, race or tribe rather than an individual. When we think of foretelling the future now, it is much more likely to be linked to us as individuals. At the moment people appear to divide into different categories:

- there are those who don't want to know the future
- others believe that it is not possible to foretell it anyway as only their own actions can create their future.
- some believe everything is pre-ordained and therefore it doesn't matter what they think or do, as in effect there is no such thing as free will and they will follow the path that has already been set for them.
- some believe that all actions are as a result of cause and effect, in which case foretelling the future is not possible because there are too many variables
- others find a kind of reassurance in seeking answers to the future.

A little later in the chapter we will explore some of the many ways in which foretelling the future can be undertaken but first a word of caution. For those who seek answers by calling upon the services of someone or something, the question should be asked *'why do I want to know and what am I going to do when I have been given an answer?'*

Seeking answers to the future can be incredibly dangerous—I wonder how many people have actually changed their actions to fit in with some kind of prediction they have been given—sometimes totally sub-consciously.

Ways of Foretelling the Future

If someone predicts something in one's future, it is very difficult to then dismiss or forget it. During the very early days of my delving into 'alternative' beliefs I had a tarot card reading with a practitioner (I later found out the person was a novice at their first psychic fair) who promptly told me at what age I would die. That reading was many years ago now and yet despite learning the person was a novice and probably misinterpreted the card, the date is clearly imprinted on my brain and I wonder how I will react when I reach that particular age. There is a responsibility that comes with foretelling the future and a practitioner needs to be extremely careful in the way they interpret images they see or thoughts they have and in the messages they give out.

So, having given the health warning, what are some of the key methods that have been used—and are still being used—to foretell the future? I have listed some with an explanation of the way they work.

ASTROLOGY (SEE SEPARATE CHAPTER)

I was going to include astrology in this section but the topic is not about the few lines of horoscopes shown in many of the papers. Astrology links planet alignment at the time of birth with the traits and characteristics of individuals and is complex to understand so I have decided it needs a complete chapter.

READING TEA LEAVES (TASSEOGRAPHY)

As well as using my own experience for this section, I have woven in a few comments on the methodology from two reference books I have in my own library. These are "The Complete Fortune Teller" by Francis X King and "How to predict your future" from Treasure Press.

Divination using some kind of symbols in a cup or bowl could possibly date back to the ancient Chinese and has certainly been used by such civilisations as the Greeks and Romans—the latter two by throwing the "lees" or dregs from wine goblets on to the ground and reading the symbols.

Reading tea leaves was popular from 19th century onwards but is now much less so. There could be a number of reasons for this—certainly divination methods change with fashion. However much of its decline may be down to the fact that most tea now comes in tea bags, offering less opportunity for readings other than with specialists who are keeping the older traditions alive. It is of course vital to use loose tea leaves for a reading and the tea should be of a variety that contains some larger leaves.

The cup used should ideally have a wide mouth and sloping sides. It should be a plain colour and either white or pale inside so that the leaves/patterns show up easily. The tea should be poured into the cup without using any kind of strainer. It is considered important that the person seeking the reading actually drinks the tea, leaving just enough liquid to swirl around the cup (perhaps ¼"). Methods differ but for my own reading I was asked to take the cup, swirl the liquid, gently pour off the liquid, turn the cup upside down onto the saucer and then turn it three times. Another method says the person having the reading should hold the cup in their left hand, swirl the liquid three times clockwise, making sure the liquid reaches the rim and then turn the cup upside down on the saucer so the liquid can drain to the count of seven.

If you are trying to do the reading yourself, it is important to take an overview of what you are looking at. It may not be easy to see any sharp specific symbols. Interpreting what you see comes with practice. However in the same way as when you are looking for an aura around someone, soft focus or half close your eyes. This may help you to see shapes or patterns.

If there are a great many leaves in the cup it can imply a rich, full life. A small scattering of a few leaves implies a tidy and disciplined mind.

The relationship of leaves to rim and handle are considered relevant. Leaves near the top of the rim may denote events that will happen in the near future whilst those further down may be on a longer timescale. There is a thought that symbols in the bottom of the cup can be unlucky. There is another thought that describes an 18/24 month span from rim to base of cup. Leaves and symbols near the handle are thought to represent events close to home, symbols pointing towards the handle are approaching and symbols pointing away are departing.

The symbols should not be read in complete isolation. Notice should be taken of the size, proportions, distances and clarity relative to each other and the whole picture interpreted as well as sections.

Both the books I mentioned earlier have sections giving interpretations for individual symbols.

At the time of my personal reading I made lots of notes and have just re-read these. Looking back now I can see that the total reading appears to be approx. 90% accurate, although some of the timescales were longer than originally suggested. Also the person who was doing my reading described one or two people who had died (one only a month before) and I believe they were therefore using clairvoyance in addition to just reading the leaves. I cannot therefore give any real guidance as to how much information came from each source.

READING A CRYSTAL BALL (SCRYING)

Although I have headed this section "reading a crystal ball" in reality it can be anything that has a reflective surface.

Ways of Foretelling the Future

The practice of staring into a reflective surface again goes back to ancient times. No-one can state when or where it began but, in various forms, it appears to have been used by such ancient civilisations as the Babylonians, Egyptians, Chinese and later, the Greeks. Crystal gazing has been known in Europe since 5th century and also is thought to have been used by the Mayans, Incas, North American Indians, Australian aborigines and various tribes.

The idea behind the practice is that the person scrying concentrates solely on the surface they are looking at and empties their mind so that the conscious mind switches off and there is an opportunity to turn inwards.

As you can imagine, this is an extremely difficult thing to do as our minds do not switch off easily and a great deal of practice is needed even to make the first steps. Rather than paying out for an expensive crystal ball, anyone beginning to use this practice could just as easily use a full glass of clean water or a mirror. It is about learning to switch off the conscious mind. Initially if this is achieved it is likely to only be for a few seconds but with practice this can be increased and can put one into a trance-like state.

Once mastery over the mind has been achieved, practitioners may see misty clouds, swirling colours or possibly images. Any such visions will of course need to be interpreted and therefore results can be extremely subjective.

There are books available that give interpretations for different colour clouds or different symbols seen.

TAROT AND OTHER CARD FORMATIONS SUCH AS ANGEL OR MEDICINE CARDS

Like many of the topics we have talked about, the origin of Tarot cards is shrouded in the mists of time. Their first recorded appearance is in medieval France in about 1390 but some contend that some of the cards contain pictures and imagery that could be traced back to ancient civilisations such as Babylon and Egypt. It is possible that the cards evolved as part of the secret folklore of the Romany peoples and came to Europe with them during their westward migrations.

The Tarot pack consists of 78 cards. 56, called the Minor Arcana are in 4 suits with 14 cards in each suit. Cards in each suit are numbered Ace to 10 and there are 4 court cards—King, Queen, Knight and Page. In readings the court cards often symbolise the following:

King *(the spirit)*

Queen *(the soul)*

Knight *(the ego)*

Page *(the body)*

Ways of Foretelling the Future

The suits are shown below and form the basis for our current playing cards.

Wands (now clubs) associated with enterprise and enquiry (element *fire*)

Cups (now hearts) associated with love and happiness (element *water*)

Swords (now spades) associated with strife and misfortune (element *air*)

Pentacles (now diamonds) associated with money and interest (element *earth*)

The 22 cards of the Major Arcana are very different and do not resemble anything we have today. They are numbered 0–21 and are picture cards each bearing a title, e.g., the sun, the high priestess, the fool etc. Each card represents a distinct principle, law, power or element in nature. The designs on the cards also show the life of man as joys and sorrows, happiness and despair. In his book "The Tarot Revealed" Eden Gray also states, "They indicate man's search for the wisdom which enables him to control his passion and help his transition to a higher sphere where he enters into the things of the spirit".

In a reading each of these cards has a dual meaning depending upon whether the picture is the right way up or upside down.

There are many different card layouts and ways of reading the tarot cards. They should always be read by someone else rather than a person trying to do their own reading. There is said to be a power in the cutting and shuffling of the cards by the person wanting the reading prior to handing them back to the person carrying out the reading.

Sometimes these cards are sold in the guise of fun and fortune telling but readings from these cards can be very powerful and should never be treated lightly.

For those wanting to study this subject in more detail, there are many books on the subject.

There are now many different types of cards one can purchase beside tarot cards. All will require the person wanting the reading to shuffle and cut the cards and again there will be different layouts. Whatever kind of cards are used, there will be a book giving the meanings for each card and again these will need to be interpreted by the person giving the reading.

I CHING (BOOK OF CHANGES)

I Ching has existed in some form or another for more than 3000 years. It is Chinese in origin, the oldest recorded oracle book, is regarded as a book of wisdom and has been consulted throughout time to obtain advice and answers to questions.

Ways of Foretelling the Future

In the I Ching tradition, the universe is seen as constructed of opposites—light and dark, hot and cold, birth and death—as shown in the interwoven symbols of Yin and Yang.

The two symbols used in the hexagram are a broken line and an unbroken line. A hexagram consists of six symbols, read from bottom to top. The current version of the book, containing 64 hexagrams is said to have been compiled by King Wen (died c. 1150 BC)

I Ching comes from a philosophy that man is capable of making his own destiny. It does not describe one marked path through life for an individual but recognises that there are many choices at different times and the future for any individual will depend on the choices made along the way which can change the outcome. The future therefore is always fluid.

Advice is provided by the enquirer asking a specific question and then casting whatever medium is being used to create the hexagram—this might be dice, special coins or the traditional yarrow stalks. The dice or coins are cast six times. If using a dice the number is noted and read from bottom to top in order to create the hexagram. Each odd number denotes an unbroken line, an even number a broken line. Traditional coins will have a plain side and a side showing characters. The plain side has a value of three and the character side a value of two. The total for each cast is noted in the same way as for dice and read bottom to top.

If using modern coins, the side showing a monetary value is taken to be the character side.

Once the hexagram has been created it can be read from a chart that shows all 64 possible combinations. The book "The Complete Fortune Teller" that I previously mentioned includes such definitions.

EXTRASENSORY PERCEPTION

There are a number of different forms of extrasensory perception, i.e., gaining information about an object, person, location or physical event through means other than the known senses. Brief descriptions are given below:

Clairvoyance—by seeing pictures

Clairaudience—by hearing or receiving thoughts

Clairsentience—by feeling or touch

Clairalience—through a sense of smell

Claircognizance—intrinsic knowledge. Knowing something without a physical explanation for why it is known.

CONSULTING A MEDIUM

Whilst it is certainly a use of extrasensory perception, in my opinion mediumship is quite a different form of communication and deserves its own entry.

Ways of Foretelling the Future

A medium is endeavouring to contact spirit and channel their messages to the person wanting the reading. Often it will be a member of the person's family who has died although it is possible for a medium to convey messages from a guide as well.

There are some excellent mediums who can bring comfort to people with their reassurance that the relative or friend they knew still exists in some form or another.

Some mediums are capable of working in large theatres, bringing messages to a number of people in quick succession. Others work from a platform such as a spiritualist church. There are mediums who will work at psychic fairs and give one-on-one readings regardless of the noise and bustle around them, those who provide one-on-one readings in their homes or another quiet venue and some who will offer a telephone reading.

When consulting a medium there are a number of things to think about:

- Why are you trying to get in touch?
- Are you wanting reassurance or guidance for the future?

Think carefully about any information you give to the medium. It is quite easy for someone who may not be as gifted to feed a line out fishing for the kind of answer that helps them make a comment. Don't give lots of information to the person. Some questions they ask may be very general—for example, "I seem to be getting someone whose name begins with S or F . . ." If you immediately give them a name, then they have something to lock on to but may not be getting a true message. Many people wanting a reading are vulnerable—they want to hear from a particular person and will interpret general comments to fit specific circumstances.

Particularly in a one-on-one session a really good medium will give you information without you divulging much at all. Take a notebook with you and make as many notes as you can. Some mediums will tape record the reading and give you the tape which is even better. Many mediums do not like to have a second person close by taking notes as they can pick up the vibrations of both people rather than just the one who is seeking the reading. A medium may ask to hold something from the person seeking the reading to help them lock on to a particular vibration.

Internationally well-known mediums include Derek Acorah, Tony Stockwell, Colin Fry and John Edward. If you "google" on the internet, you will find names and details.

PALMISTRY

Palmistry is also known as Chiromancy (from the Greek word "cheir" (hand). No-one knows for certain when palmistry began although like some other forms of fortune telling that we have considered, it is likely to have started in the east and travelled west. There are however references to the art that go back 3000+ years. During the 17th century attitudes to palmistry certainly varied from country to country—being taught in some German universities whilst being outlawed in England as a form of witchcraft.

There are many aspects to a palmistry reading and it is important to take an overall picture rather than concentrating on one particular feature. The lines on an individual's hand can be quite different to those shown in illustrations and it takes a lot of experience to provide successful readings.

The following features will be taken into account in a reading:

- shape of hand and hand span
- shape of nails
- nail colour
- finger shapes, flexibility and bend of individual fingers
- lines (key lines are head line, heart line, line of fate, life line and line of the sun)
- mounts (fleshy pads at base of fingers, thumb etc.)
- marks and textures

Maggie Clements

There is a belief that the left hand shows the potentialities an individual was born with and the right hand reveals the person's nature as it is now and what the future may be. (the reverse applies for left handed people).

CHAPTER 14

Astrology

Astrology has been studied for many centuries and as with many of the topics discussed in the previous chapter, was used to try to predict events important to the various civilisations.

The Greeks were one of the first to create an astronomical table charting the position of each planet for each day of the year. Originally the study of astrology was closely aligned to that of astronomy because of the significance of the stars.

Modern astrology has moved to become person-centred and underlines a belief that people are influenced by the sun, moon and eight of the planets. The eight planets are Mercury, Venus, Mars, Jupiter, Saturn, Uranus, Neptune and Pluto. The twelve signs of the zodiac create the vehicle by which calculations are made and an astrological birth chart will consider the exact position of sun, moon and each planet in relation to the zodiac signs at the time of birth. For the purpose of these calculations, earth is taken to be at the centre with the planets revolving around it.

The theory is that the sun, moon and each planet will exert an influence and therefore encourage certain personality traits within an individual. In this way astrology provides an insight into the character of an individual, and potential characteristics they may be able to develop during their life. It is not as much about foretelling the future.

At first glance this can seem a far-fetched theory. However if one pauses for a moment to consider the natural influence the sun and moon alone have on the earth the idea can become more constructive.

The sun is incredibly powerful and throws out mass coronal ejections into space from violent storms on its surface. When these are facing earth, enormous bursts of radiation are transmitted towards us, often resulting in issues with satellites, communication and atmospheric events such as "aurora" or in our hemisphere "the northern lights" being seen—sometimes to quite a wide latitude. The sun is not a constant in terms of its energy in that from science we know it has an eleven year cycle. The influence of this radiation and solar storms on the earth will therefore be very different at various points of that cycle.

We are also very aware of the moon's influence on our planet, for example the height of the tides are strongly affected by its gravitational pull as well as by the time of year. The moon is like the sun in that its influence is variable—there are times when its orbit brings it very close to us and others when it is much further away, altering the effect.

For an astrological chart to be accurately drawn up for an individual, certain information needs to be available. Ideally the person needs to be able to provide the date, the hour of their birth and the place of birth so that the exact co-ordinates can be identified. The person (or computer) drawing up the chart can then calculate from astronomical tables the exact position of each of the planets against the signs of the zodiac.

In addition to calculating the position of each planet, there are four other readings that are considered to be important. The most commonly recognised one is the Sun Sign. In other words, the zodiac sign ruling at the time of birth. This is believed to have a key influence on the individual. The others considered to have a key influence are:

Rising Sign (ascendant)

This is the zodiac sign on the horizon at the time of birth. It is believed this will have almost the same level of influence as the Sun Sign and therefore the vast majority of people will have a combination of characteristics from the two signs.

In much rarer cases (less than 1%) the Rising Sign and the Sun Sign will be in the same sign of the zodiac and these are considered to strengthen and emphasise the one set of characteristics.

The Sign the moon is in

The mid heaven sign

This is the highest above the horizon at the time of birth

According to the book, *How to predict your future*:

"The traditional body of knowledge used by astrologers to describe personality traits comes from ancient mythology, centuries of observation and adaptation and now includes ideas from analytical psychology"

I have just provided the barest outline of astrology as a subject. It does of course investigate many other features of the zodiac signs including:

Astrology

The three qualities of the signs (or mode)

Cardinal (initiating—use abilities to achieve ambitions)

Fixed (persistent—hold on to what they have and can resist change)

Mutable (flexible—always searching and often changing)

The four elements

Fire (enthusiastic—not easy to contain—once burning will use up air, boil water and scorch earth)

Earth (practical—can be used for building or planting—can channel water, make a place for fire and co-exist with air)

Air (cerebral—always on the move—can rise above earth, bubble water and essential for fire)

Water (sensitivity—seeks own level and exists in several states—can put out fire, flood earth and dampen air)

The three qualities of the houses

Angular (where action is initiated)

Succedent (where action is stabilised)

Cadent (where we learn from actions and adapt)

The four house elements

Houses of life (boundless energy, enthusiasm and conviction)

Houses of purpose (stable, reliable and practical)

Houses of relationships (need other people)

Houses of endings (sensitive to the way we attain freedom)

Aspects

Conjunction	0°
Opposition	180°
Trine	120°
Square	90°
Sextile	60°

Just to finish this chapter, the following is from an astrological chart I had drawn up by Equinox of London

Signs

Aries	I am
Taurus	I have
Gemini	I think
Cancer	I feel

Astrology

Leo	I will
Virgo	I analyse
Libra	I balance
Scorpio	I desire
Sagittarius	I seek
Capricorn	I use
Aquarius	I know
Pisces	I believe

CHAPTER 15

Mind, Body, Spirit

Throughout the preceding chapters we have been looking at various aspects of mind, body, spirit.

In some cases we have been thinking about mental approaches and how to keep a level of mindfulness in everything we do. In this way we can recognise that we have choices about how we think and the attitudes and approaches we take.

In other chapters we have concentrated on the physical aspects of life—how to maintain energy and help to keep the body at its maximum to self-heal etc.

We have also concentrated on how to improve our ability to grow and develop skills and abilities via meditation and channelling energy.

We have also explored how one aspect in our lives can affect another. For example, if you are mentally uneasy about something—even if this has been pushed to the back of your mind and into the subconscious—it will have a physical effect on your body and there will be signs of illness.

It is now time to put these three aspects together and recognise that there is a total relationship between them. Mental, physical and spiritual development goes hand-in-hand, and once working in harmony can change your life totally.

Recognising the connection between them and using the connections mindfully will allow you to live within a constant flow of good energy. You will be connected to everything around you, giving energy to it and taking energy from it but not in a negative way that causes any issues for anyone else. This state allows you to stay in a positive and energised frame of mind with the ability to help others without taking energy away from yourself.

Maintaining this kind of approach in our lives can be very difficult. Our world can be full of stresses and pressures and sometimes these can become so big in our minds that we get pushed off track and diverted into a much more personal and "narrow" thought pattern. This can become a habit and at such times we can become mentally separated from our higher thoughts, feeling worried and that we are battling tough times in our lives and alone. These

Mind, Body, Spirit

can be very testing times and drain all our energy so that we feel we are just existing. It can be difficult to change mind-set, but the sooner you recognise what is happening and go back to a different mental approach, the sooner you will be able to improve your life again. Remember how you think is your choice. Taking a more positive mind-set and affirming a different future will help it to happen.

Once you become used to aligning mind, body and spirit, you are likely to experience a much happier, smoother and more positive life. You are likely to stay healthier with an improved sense of wellbeing. Once your own life is in this kind of state, it becomes so much easier to make decisions, live life to the full and help other people.

Alignment brings a peace of mind and knowledge that everything that happens is happening for the right reasons and in the way intended. It is difficult to describe how good it feels when one is "connected" but it brings with it a sense that one is never alone. Should you need someone to talk to at any time and you do not wish to share thoughts with a friend, find somewhere quiet and talk to "spirit". Once you are connected you can always be helped. As I mentioned in an earlier chapter, spirit will never intervene without being asked but once invited to help, there is a clear feeling of comfort and support.

Maggie Clements

We are truly never alone unless we choose to be. You are constantly a part of a "whole universe" and can live your life in the sure knowledge that if you do your best, events will happen that will be relevant and helpful to what you want to achieve.

About the Author

Maggie Clements is married and lives in South Cambridgeshire with her husband. She has worked all her life—in both private and public sectors and for the past 20 years has run her own Training and HR Consultancy.

She first became interested in what is sometimes referred to as "alternative thinking" approximately 30 years' ago when she undertook a course of evening classes on various topics.

Since that time she has pursued a number of activities which include working as a volunteer healer at a holistic centre, working one-on-one with people who need help or guidance to help them overcome mental or physical problems, meeting specialists in various subjects to develop her own skills and training others. She has studied hands on healing, is a Reiki Master and a qualified Thought Field Therapist.

People she has met often tell her that her enthusiasm and down to earth practical approach to discussing a wide range of topics help them to have a belief and she is recognised as someone who helps people begin their learning and development. She has written First Footsteps in the hope that it will act as a guide to people who want to start learning about these fascinating subjects.

>www.amethystdevelopmentbooks.co.uk
>www.amethystdevelopmentbooks.com

www.ingramcontent.com/pod-product-compliance
Lightning Source LLC
Chambersburg PA
CBHW050539300426
44113CB00012B/2183